The Transforming Power of Forgiveness

Philip Nunn

Scripture Truth Publications

THE TRANSFORMING POWER OF FORGIVENESS

FIRST EDITION
FIRST PRINTING January 2012
Typeset and transferred to Digital Printing 2011
ISBN: 978-0-901860-91-0 (paperback)
Copyright © 2011 Philip Nunn and Scripture Truth Publications in this edition

All rights reserved. No part of this publication may be reproduced, stored in a retrieval system, or transmitted, in any form or by any means, electronic, mechanical, photocopying, recording or otherwise without prior permission of Scripture Truth Publications.

Scripture quotations, unless otherwise indicated, are taken from the New King James Version®. Copyright © 1982 by Thomas Nelson, Inc. Used by permission. All rights reserved.
Scripture quotations marked (N.Tr.) are taken from "The Holy Scriptures, a New Translation from the Original Languages" by J. N. Darby (G Morrish, 1890)
Scripture quotations marked (NIV) are taken from
The Holy Bible, New International Version (Anglicised edition)
Copyright © 1979, 1984, 2011 by Biblica (formerly International Bible Society).
Used by permission of Hodder & Stoughton Publishers, an Hachette UK company
All rights reserved.
'NIV' is a registered trademark of Biblica (formerly International Bible Society).
UK trademark number 1448790.
Scripture quotations marked (ESV) are from The Holy Bible, English Standard Version® (ESV®), copyright © 2001 by Crossway, a publishing ministry of Good News Publishers. Used by permission. All rights reserved.

Cover illustration ©iStockphoto.com/Liliboas (Lisa Thornberg)

German Edition: ISBN 978-3-935955-45-4 © 2010 Daniel-Verlag, www.daniel-verlag.de
Dutch Edition: ISBN 978-90-79465-16-3 © 2011 Heart Cry, www.heartcry.nl

Published by Scripture Truth Publications
31-33 Glover Street,
Crewe, Cheshire, CW1 3LD
Scripture Truth is an imprint of Central Bible Hammond Trust, a charitable trust
Typesetting by John Rice
Printed and bound by Lightning Source

THE TRANSFORMING POWER OF FORGIVENESS

Contents

About this book 7
Foreword – Glass in your arm! 9
Part One: Heart forgiveness sets you free . 13
What is forgiveness? 16
It is time to forgive! 17
A time to ask for forgiveness 18
What happens if we do not forgive? 20
The Biblical basis for forgiveness 22
Reasons to postpone forgiving 25
Forgiveness, justice or revenge 29
Misunderstandings about forgiveness 30
Forgiveness and bitterness 33
When a believer cannot forgive 35
What is involved in forgiving? 38
People who did not forgive 40
   Mephibosheth 40
   Jephthah 41
   Samson 43
People who did forgive 45
   A Jewish young lady 45
   Joseph 46
Steps to freedom 48
First prayer 49
Second prayer 50

PART TWO: WHEN SHOULD I FORGIVE? 51
CHOOSING THE RIGHT TIME TO FORGIVE 53
POSSIBLE DIFFICULTIES 54
A WORD CAN MEAN DIFFERENT THINGS 56
THE BIBLE'S USE OF THE WORD "FORGIVENESS" 57
   1. aphiemi 57
   2. apoluo 58
   3. aphesis 58
   4. charizomai 59
DIFFERENT TYPES OF FORGIVENESS 60
   1. Legal Forgiveness 61
     How to receive God's Legal Forgiveness 62
   2. Fatherly Forgiveness 63
GOD'S FORGIVENESS IS A MODEL FOR OUR
   FORGIVENESS 65
DIFFERENT RELATIONSHIPS THAT NEED TO BE
   RESTORED 66
   3. Church Forgiveness 69
   4. Governmental Forgiveness 70
   5. Heart Forgiveness 71
     Heart Forgiveness, before the offender repents? 73
     What next? 75
   6. Relational Forgiveness 76
     Saying "I forgive you" 77
WHEN NOT TO HOLD BACK CHURCH
   AND RELATIONAL FORGIVENESS 78

THE TRANSFORMING POWER OF FORGIVENESS

Reconciliation 81
A growing celebration 82
Reconciliation, forgiveness and justice 83
7. Self-Forgiveness 84
Summary table 87
Conclusion 88

About This Book

Forgiveness is an important theme in Scripture. When I was somewhat younger, I would teach and preach about forgiveness. I would show from Scripture that as Christians we should forgive those who sin against us. Brothers and sisters would agree with me, thank me for the 'good message' but then nothing much would happen. The grudges and the bitterness would remain under the surface. The act of forgiveness would not take place.

In counselling situations during my last years in Colombia, I experienced great joy in leading believers step by step to forgive unfaithful husbands, controlling mothers, irresponsible fathers, acts of aggression, rape, theft and religious manipulation. I am really enthusiastic about this theme of forgiveness because it is Biblical and I have seen firsthand its transforming power.

After working with my wife in Colombia as Christian missionaries for 15 years, we returned to Europe. Here I continue to teach and encourage forgiveness. But unlike in Colombia, where my audience were mainly first and second generation Christians, here most of my listeners came from families who have been Christian for many generations. I was surprised to discover that many of these Christians find it much more difficult to forgive. They agree in principle that forgiveness is necessary, but have developed many 'doctrinal' and 'logical' arguments to postpone forgiveness. This book is my response. In it you will find not only Biblical answers and explanations, but also a strong motivation to act now – namely, to forgive!

This book is made up of two parts. You will notice a difference in style between these two parts, the first being more conversational. Part One is based on the recordings of two seminars given at Reconvillier (Switzerland) in June 2008. Here, forgiveness is presented from a Christian pastoral perspective. It explores why forgiveness is necessary and states that forgiveness must always be given freely as an act of grace. No-one deserves to be forgiven. After correcting some misunderstandings that hinder the act of forgiveness it moves on to explain and motivate "forgiveness from the heart". At the end of Part One you will be encouraged to put into practice this Biblical teaching and forgive from your heart anyone who has hurt you.

Our heavenly Father always forgives repentant sinners. Should Christian victims only forgive their offenders if they repent? When humans forgive are they doing the same thing as when God forgives? Could it be that the Bible uses the word 'forgive' to describe related but different activities? These and other questions are explored in Part Two. You don't have to understand all the Biblical teaching about forgiveness before you can forgive. Like salvation, even children can enjoy the peace and freedom that come through simple obedience.

If you are searching for a Biblical understanding of forgiveness or are involved in Bible teaching, Christian counselling or have a heart to help others experience the transforming power of forgiveness, you will find in Part Two a collection of challenging and useful ideas.

Foreword - Glass in your arm!

Imagine the situation where a young man falls through a glass window. At the hospital they clean his wounded arm, but by mistake leave a sharp splinter of glass imbedded in his arm. With care and time, the arm will heal nicely on the outside. Soon he will be able to move his arm nearly as freely as before the accident. He is happy to be nearly normal again. But soon he will discover one or two movements that cause him a great deal of pain. Such movements make him want to stop and scream!

Those who have not forgiven somebody walk around with a sharp piece of glass in their arm. The presence of glass becomes obvious when a person 'jumps' or displays an abnormally strong reaction to a particular topic, situation or person. If a young man has not forgiven his dominant mother who regularly yelled at him, he is likely to be very sensitive to those who scream and to those in authority. If a young woman has not forgiven the unknown man who tried to rape her in the park, she may no longer be able to enjoy a walk in a park and will find it very uncomfortable to watch a film where a woman walks alone at night. She may try to stop the film or walk out. Something has touched the glass in her arm.

What is the solution? Some secular psychotherapists may help by identifying your painful movements and teach you how to live avoiding those movements. Following their advice will reduce your pain. But that is not the Christian way. The Lord Jesus invites His followers to "forgive from the heart", to remove the glass. It will require cutting the arm open and removing the foreign object. The process may well be very painful. For a while the arm may bleed again. But this is the only way, it is Christ's way, to restore normal movement to the arm.

Can we forget? As long as the glass remains in our arm, we shall experience regular painful reminders of the offence. We shall never be able to forget. Once we forgive from our heart, the glass is removed. In time our arm will heal and full movement will return. Some experiences we shall never forget. The scar on our arm will stay with us to our dying day. But after we have forgiven from our heart, the pain connected with the memory will gradually decrease. A time will come, perhaps sooner than you expect, when you will notice that the Lord has healed you to such an extent that you no longer feel any pain when thinking about the offence. Through forgiveness the Lord has healed you. In fact, after we choose to obey the Lord Jesus and forgive the undeserving offender with all our heart, the irritation, the anger, the pain, the desire for revenge will begin to give way to a mixture of sadness, concern, pity and compassion towards the unrepentant offending person.

Do you perhaps have glass in your arm? Do you want to help someone who does? The practical Bible teaching in

FOREWORD – GLASS IN YOUR ARM!

this book will help you remove glass from hurting arms, so that we may all function freely and happily in the Master's service. Healed arms build and bless others.

Part One

Heart Forgiveness Sets You Free

Heart Forgiveness Sets You Free

One of the biggest problems among Christians, as far as I can observe, is the lack of forgiveness. The Christian community has its share of problems, including occasional financial and sexual scandals. The lack of forgiveness is recognized by most, but few consider it a scandal. And yet it acts like poison in our churches, ministries and communities. When we meet brothers and sisters who display signs of bitterness, we empathize – we try to explain and justify their hard attitude, odd behaviour or sharp words. We are told that "she has been through a very difficult time", or "he has been treated very unfairly at work or at church". We are urged to understand and accept their odd behaviour as normal in view of something painful they have lived through in the past. We no longer consider the lack of forgiveness and the resulting bitterness as sin.

Is it true that the Lord Jesus came to set captives free? Does this mean that every Christian actually lives and enjoys that freedom? The Lord Jesus has removed the locks from our chains and opened the prison doors. The Lord Jesus has made us free, but we still cling to our chains! We remain in bondage, not because the blood of Jesus was not powerful enough to free us, but because we do not let go of those chains, because we do not walk out and enter into that freedom.

What is forgiveness?

What actually happens when someone becomes a Christian? I first realize and accept that I am a sinner. I come to the Lord Jesus and ask Him to forgive me. I hand myself over completely to Him, and He gladly receives me. I am now born again – I have begun a new life. Which of my sins are forgiven when I am born again? All my sins are forgiven – those I have committed in the past but also those that I am going to commit in the future. The simple reality is that when the Lord Jesus died on the cross, all my sins were still future sins. When I became a Christian, I received from the Lord complete forgiveness. All my sins are forgiven, past and future. I am totally forgiven! Some call this Legal Forgiveness.

There is, however, another aspect of forgiveness, which some refer to as Fatherly Forgiveness. If I as a Christian sin, something happens between me and my heavenly Father. The communion, the harmony we enjoy with Him, is broken. The apostle John tells us how this communion can be restored: "If we confess our sins, He is faithful and just to forgive us our sins" (1 John 1:9). Notice that this verse does not say that God is 'loving and kind'. This is clearly true, but the forgiveness of our sins is not based on His loving kindness. We can be forgiven because on the cross Jesus Christ paid the penalty for our sin and God the Father is "faithful and just" to apply the benefit of Christ's work on our behalf. Once I confess a sin to Him, I receive His Fatherly Forgiveness.

WHAT IS FORGIVENESS?

If I am a Christian, I have received God's Legal Forgiveness for all my sins. When I sin as a child of God, I will also need His Fatherly Forgiveness. Because I have received Legal Forgiveness, my position before God is firm, my salvation is secure. But what can vary from day to day is my enjoyment of Him and of that firm salvation. Through Fatherly Forgiveness the enjoyment of my heavenly Father is restored.

What happens after I sin? Consider the parable of the Prodigal Son. When he finally recognized what he had done and where he was, he said to himself, "I will arise and go to my father, and will say to him, 'Father, I have sinned against heaven and against you'" (Luke 15:18). He had sinned against heaven and against his father. When we sin we also usually harm two parties: we sin against a fellow human and at the same time we also sin against our heavenly Father. In order to set the matter right, we must confess our sin to our heavenly Father and He will grant us His Fatherly Forgiveness. But we must not forget the horizontal element – we must also seek to fix the damage we have caused to our fellow human.

IT IS TIME TO FORGIVE!

What do you intend to do with this book? Do you only want to improve your Biblical knowledge about forgiveness? I hope not! My prayer is that as you read these pages and reflect on its content the Holy Spirit will bring to your mind those who have hurt you, those you need to forgive. May your time spent with this book be a time of forgiveness. Can you imagine yourself completely free from that frustrating, annoying or painful past? The Lord wants you to let go of your chains and walk out free. He has paid a high price to secure your freedom and He wants you now to enjoy that freedom to the full!

Just think for a moment! Who is that person who has really hurt you? Some of you are probably thinking of your father or your mother. Perhaps they are old now or perhaps they have been dead for a number of years. But you still feel hot and angry when you remember how he or she treated you. Perhaps you are thinking of a brother or a sister in your local church. If we take our Christian life and our local Church seriously, unjustified or exaggerated criticism by fellow believers hurts very badly. Unfortunately, such events are not rare! Sometimes we Christians can spend many years holding on to those chains.

A TIME TO ASK FOR FORGIVENESS

Have you ever sinned against someone else? It is easy to think of those situations where others have sinned against us. We shall return to this situation shortly, but first ask yourself these questions: Is there someone I have hurt? Did I say something to somebody with an angry or despising tone in my voice? Have I written a letter or an e-mail with words that could have hurt another? Maybe you're thinking: "Yes, but he deserves it! Perhaps I have exaggerated a little, but 80 per cent of what I wrote is true. At least I was honest!" You can hold on to your excuse, you can repeat it to yourself a thousand times, but that will not set you free. You must confess your 20 per cent. The only way to walk free is to acknowledge your share in the problem and confess your sin.

When I was quite young I learnt this lesson. One of my hobbies was to collect coins. One day I visited one of my cousins in Holland, who also had a coin collection, a much larger one than my own. She had a number of repeated coins, including a small but interesting coin from Luxembourg, which I had not got. When no-one was looking, I quietly slipped it into my pocket. When we returned home – we were living in England at that time – I put the coin in my collection. But soon I began to feel guilty about what I had done. I would tell myself that my cousin had lots of coins and would not miss it. That it was one of her repeated coins and therefore she did not really need it. That it was a small coin and that it was really of very little value. I reasoned that if I would have asked her for it, I was pretty sure that she would have given it to me. With such arguments I would convince myself for a while. But my internal restlessness would soon return. I simply felt too embarrassed to contact my cousin and explain what I had done.

After a week or two I took the coin out of my collection and put it somewhere in the garage. Now I would no longer see the coin, in fact, I was no longer in possession of it – but my conscience was still not at rest. I became very frustrated with myself. How could I have been so foolish as to take that coin home? I was not free. It was only an insignificant little coin but it was destroying my joy during the day and making me restless at night. What could I do? Eventually I wrote a short explanatory letter, stuck the coin to it and put it in the post. Now I was free again! It felt so good!

What kind of letter should you take to the post office today? It is worth the embarrassment, because after you send it you are free. The personal frustration associated with the embarrassment is also very useful – it helps us not to do it again! Right now I would like to encourage you, stronger still, I would like to urge you in the name of Jesus to set things right: if you have hurt someone in your family, perhaps your mother, your father, your son or your daughter – decide now to apologize and set things right. If you have said, done or written something harmful to a brother, do not justify your action by reasoning: "Oh yes, he is a very difficult brother, he has hurt many other people too!" That may be true, but that is his problem! If you have done something wrong to him, then confess your sin, clean your side. My dear brother, my dear sister, it is so nice to live the freedom that Christ has purchased for us! The enjoyment of your freedom may be just a phone call, a letter or an e-mail away. Do it and you will be free! But please, do it right now!

In Psalm 32 David writes about a frustrating experience. He probably thought that by simply waiting the problem would go away or disappear, so he chose to keep silent. "When I kept silent, my bones grew old through my groaning all the day long. For day and night Your hand was heavy upon me" (verses 3-4). Then he found the solution: "I acknowledged my sin to You, and my iniquity I have not hidden. I said, 'I will confess my transgressions to the LORD,' and You forgave the iniquity of my sin" (verse 5). Do you want to enjoy that freedom again? Honest confession is the only way!

WHAT HAPPENS IF WE DO NOT FORGIVE?

Now let's consider the other side. What happens when someone has sinned against you? It is precisely the same: he or she has sinned not only against you but also against God. The offender must set things right with both God and you.

Why is forgiveness so important? Let's turn a moment to the Lord's prayer which He taught during the Sermon on the Mount as recorded by Matthew. He began the

WHAT HAPPENS IF WE DO NOT FORGIVE?

prayer with the words: "Our Father in heaven," and a little later He continues, "Forgive us our debts." And why or how? – "as we forgive our debtors." At the end of the prayer the Lord Jesus says something that is simple to understand and yet for some Bible students quite difficult to harmonize with other Scriptures: "But if you do not forgive men their trespasses, neither will your Father forgive your trespasses" (Matthew 6:9-15).

It is a serious matter if we do not forgive. It is an imperative for us Christians to learn to forgive one another. "And do not grieve the Holy Spirit of God, by whom you were sealed for the day of redemption. Let all bitterness, wrath, anger, clamor, and evil speaking be put away from you, with all malice. And be kind to one another, tenderhearted, forgiving one another, just as God in Christ forgave you" (Ephesians 4:30-32).

If someone has sinned against us and we refuse to forgive, then something happens in the spiritual world: we restrict the freedom of the Holy Spirit and grieve Him. Oh yes, we can still sing hymns, but the Holy Spirit is grieved. We can still take part at the Lord's Supper, but the Holy Spirit is grieved. Yes, we can still talk about the Bible, preach the Word and participate in good Christian activities. But as we do so, we shall be playing a Christian game, we shall lack reality.

Children like to play. Sometimes you see small children playing Mothers and Fathers. Sometimes they play being a family, giving a lesson at school or buying and selling in a shop. Sometimes children from Christian homes play church meetings; they can play baptisms and even the Lord's Supper. I remember playing such games with my two brothers. Children imitate what they see.

But even as adults we can sometimes just follow our comfortable customs and play church. And we can do so because our conscience has become hardened by lack of forgiveness. We know that if we don't forgive someone, our prayers will be hindered. But we hold on to an offence and harbour some anger towards that offending person and think that we can continue to pray as if nothing negative happens in the spiritual realm. Neither you nor I are exceptions. These spiritual rules revealed in God's Word hold true for all of us.

THE BIBLICAL BASIS FOR FORGIVENESS

What follows is the basis for forgiveness as recorded for us in Matthew chapter 18.

"Then Peter came to Him and said, 'Lord, how often shall my brother sin against me, and I forgive him? Up to seven times?' Jesus said to him, 'I do not say to you, up to seven times, but up to seventy times seven. Therefore the kingdom of heaven is like a certain king who wanted to settle accounts with his servants. And when he had begun to settle accounts, one was brought to him who owed him ten thousand talents. But as he was not able to pay, his master commanded that he be sold, with his wife and children and all that he had, and that payment be made. The servant therefore fell down before him, saying, "Master, have patience with me, and I will pay you all." Then the master of that servant was moved with compassion, released him, and forgave him the debt. But that servant went out and found one of his fellow servants who owed him a hundred denarii; and he laid hands on him and took him by the throat, saying, "Pay me what you owe!" So his fellow servant fell down at his feet and begged him, saying, "Have patience with me, and I will pay you all." And he would not, but

THE BIBLICAL BASIS FOR FORGIVENESS

went and threw him into prison till he should pay the debt. So when his fellow servants saw what had been done, they were very grieved, and came and told their master all that had been done. Then his master, after he had called him, said to him, "You wicked servant! I forgave you all that debt because you begged me. Should you not also have had compassion on your fellow servant, just as I had pity on you?" And his master was angry, and delivered him to the torturers until he should pay all that was due to him. So My heavenly Father also will do to you if each of you, from his heart, does not forgive his brother his trespasses'"(Matthew 18:21-35).

This is an interesting little parable. For a short moment, try to imagine yourself as the king in the parable. Imagine that someone owes you a huge sum of money. He is no longer meeting his repayment obligations and is falling further and further behind. He has reached the state where he can't even pay the interest on the debt. One day he comes humbly to you and says in desperation: "I'm sorry; I just can't pay you back." Then you, as a kind king, look at him and say: "Yes, I know you really can't pay me back. The sum is too large. I have decided to cancel the totality of your debt. You may now go home."

Did this man deserve that you should cancel his debt? No-one deserves forgiveness. Forgiveness is always an act of grace – it must always be given freely and voluntarily. Notice that the king did not say, "I will forgive 98 per cent of your debt, and please sign this repayment programme for the remaining 2 per cent." No! Christian forgiveness is always free and complete forgiveness.

My dear sister, my dear brother, the beginning of this parable is a vivid and emotional illustration of our conversion, when we came in desperation to the Lord Jesus seeking forgiveness and salvation. Some of us were more aware of the magnitude of our debt than others. We were all condemned sinners but some were more conscious of their sin than others. Are you aware of the huge size of the debt that has been forgiven? Some Christians are unaware of the filthiness of their own sin. They are thankful but they think they have been forgiven little. Once we become aware of the magnitude of the debt which Jesus has cancelled for us, our hearts will begin to soften and we shall become a little more prepared to follow that generous example, and also forgive the debts of others.

Think carefully about this. Whatever someone else has done to offend you, the debt is small compared to what you have done to offend God. God knows all about you. He is aware of each one of your bad thoughts. Maybe you're thinking: "Oh, I have never killed anyone", but perhaps you were once so angry you would have liked to! Or, "I have never had an adulterous relationship", but sometimes you have found the idea quite interesting – you haven't, only because you are afraid of possible negative consequences. God knows your thoughts; He knows all the places and websites you have visited. The blood of Jesus Christ has completely cleansed you from all this filth. This is the wonderful freedom that Christ has purchased for us. And now the Lord Jesus says to you, "Because I have forgiven you so much, I want you to go and forgive your brother and your sister."

In this parable the king is deeply disappointed with the forgiven servant who did not want to forgive his fellow servant. He says, in other words, "Look, I have just forgiven you an impossible debt of millions, why can't you have the kindness of heart and forgive another one hundred denarii?" It is true that this person has hurt you, she has said something untrue about you, he has stolen something from you. What he or she has done is wrong, it is sin, it is a real debt. It is not a matter of pretending the debt is smaller, nor of making evil deeds look less evil. Sin is sin. A debt is a debt. The point is that all inter-human debts are small compared with the way you and I have offended God. In this parable Jesus says so. And He knows what He is talking about.

What does God expect us to do? The king said, "Shouldn't you have had mercy on your fellow-servant just as I had on you?" We are to forgive others freely and voluntarily. Forgiveness is always an undeserved gift. Jesus ends His parable by urging all Christians to "forgive your brother from your heart".

REASONS TO POSTPONE FORGIVING

It puzzles me when I hear a Christian say something like, "Yes, of course I will forgive him, but only after he repents and then comes and asks me to forgive him." In Luke 17:3 the Lord Jesus said, "If your brother sins against you, rebuke him; and if he repents, forgive him." So I wait. Since this difficult brother who split our happy local church has not yet repented, I must patiently hold back my forgiveness. And that carnal sister, who spoke evil of my husband twenty years ago, still shows no sign of repentance. Therefore I have not forgiven her. But, I am a spiritual Christian; I am prepared to forgive her immediately as soon as she shows true signs of repentance.

About 18 months ago I attended a youth camp in Colombia. As I spoke I noticed a young man in his early twenties who was unusually distracted during the Bible studies. He was not his normal cheerful and attentive self. During a break I took him aside and asked him what was wrong. He stared sadly at the floor and said: "Last Friday my sister was raped. On her way home from work she has to walk along a fairly quiet street. Two young men grabbed her, put a paper bag over her head, dragged her into the bushes next to the road, and then raped her. Since she came home I can't get this out of my mind. I think about it over and over again. I feel very angry, I would like to find and kill these men." I listened quietly and said nothing. I shared a little of his pain.

If you have a sister or a daughter you can probably imagine the internal turmoil of this young man. If you are a woman, you may well imagine the explosive range of emotions that the young lady must have experienced, from shame and helplessness to anger and a desire for revenge. But life goes on. What options are now available to this young man and his sister? Should they wait for repentance before considering forgiveness? Knowing the situation in Colombia, it is unlikely that these two men will be found and brought to justice. What is the possibility that these two rapists will turn up repentant at her house and say "please forgive us for the wrong we have done"? Of course, with God everything is possible, but this scenario is extremely unlikely.

What should this young woman do? What should her Christian parents and brother do? If they let the weeks go by and do nothing, they can be bound to this painful event for ten, twenty, forty or more years. What happened that Friday evening can have a profound effect on the future happiness of the whole family. For that young woman, it could affect the way she sees men. Every time she gets close to something romantic, the memories of that Friday evening come back, together with its anger, shame and other negative emotions. She freezes. If she marries, she will probably find it difficult to enjoy intimacy with her husband, her mind and emotions jumping back to that first time.

No, dear sister, dear brother, let us not wait until our offenders ask us to forgive them. We should forgive them from our heart before they ask – even if they have no intention of repenting!

(If you find that this advice conflicts with your understanding of Scriptures, I suggest you stop reading this chapter, mark this page, and first read Part Two of this book. You will benefit more from the rest of Part One if you can first answer your honest intellectual doubts about when we are called to forgive.)

We had a number of counselling sessions with another 26 year old young man in Colombia, the son of Christian parents. When he was 13 years old he began taking drugs. He came to our church seeking help because he was desperate. Together with another brother we spent two or three afternoons talking with him about forgiveness, trying to show him from the Bible how important this is. He wrote down a list with the names of all those who had deeply hurt him over the years, a list that included his father. Then we started praying. He went down the list, one name at a time, praying and forgiving them in the name of Jesus. Finally we came to the last name on his list. Although he was a rather rough and tough type of young man, he broke down and began to weep. He stopped praying and said: "No, not this one. I can't forgive him. I promised myself I would some day kill him." We asked him to explain such strong emotions. This was the man who had introduced him to the drug scene.

"When I was a boy," he said, "this guy always gave me free drugs. He got me hooked. He has ruined my life. He must someday pay for this. I'm going to kill him… But if I forgive him, I can't kill him… So I can't forgive him."

We explained to him that this man had sinned not only against him but also against God. In his frustration and anger this young man thought that if he forgave the drug dealer, the man would be completely free. That would not be fair. It conflicted with his sense of justice. But God is the final judge. No-one and nothing escapes His attention. Even after we have forgiven, the offender will still have to give an account of his offence to God. But God calls us to forgive.

Look at it this way, forgiveness involves cutting a rope that ties us to someone. It involves putting an end to our personal claim. In the name of Jesus we consciously decide to 'let go'. When we forgive, we are set free.

One of my neighbours in Colombia once asked me to lend him some money. He wanted to buy a new TV. He explained that he would pay me back the following week. I lent him about 30 dollars. But the following week nothing happened. Every day he used to walk past our corner house to catch this bus to work. But from that day on he walked around the other side of the block to catch his bus. He avoided contact with us. A month passed, two months, and nothing happened. Every time I saw or heard him I thought: "Oh, there goes my 30 dollars. Does he think I am stupid or that I have forgotten? What is going to happen to my 30 dollars?" In some cultures it is not so easy to talk directly about these money matters. If I raised the issue with him, he would feel threatened or humiliated by me, especially so because I am European. Finally I realized I faced a simple choice: to forgive him or to damage the relationship with my neighbours. So I forgave him in my heart. I did not just mentally forgive the debt of 30 dollars, but in the name of Jesus I also forgave his unpleasant attitude towards us. Then I could see him again as a normal neighbour. He still had a problem, but not with me. Forgiving him set me free to behave normally towards my neighbours.

FORGIVENESS, JUSTICE OR REVENGE

In the Old Testament we find a man named Zechariah. The people disliked the message the Lord gave him to share and decided to stone him to death. "Then the Spirit of God came upon Zechariah son of Jehoiada the priest, who stood above the people, and said to them, 'Thus says God: "Why do you transgress the commandments of the LORD, so that you cannot prosper? Because you have forsaken the LORD, He also has forsaken you."' So they conspired against him, and at the command of the king they stoned him with stones in the court of the house of the LORD. Thus Joash the king did not remember the kindness which Jehoiada his father had done to him, but killed his son; and as he died, he said, 'The LORD look on it, and repay!'" (2 Chronicles 24:20-22). Notice the last words of this man while he was being killed. It was a call for justice. This is an Old Testament reaction.

What did the Lord Jesus say when He was being killed? Did He call for justice? No. The Jewish leaders, the Roman soldiers, the ungrateful and curious multitude showed no sign of repentance. Clearly most were not aware of what was really going on. Quite often people who offend and hurt others are not aware of the damage they are causing. Our New Testament model response is that of our Lord Jesus: "Father, forgive them …" (Luke 23:34).

Some years later, Stephen was stoned to death. This must have been a cruel and ugly way to die: he had been on trial before the high priest and the council and a crowd of Jews. After Stephen explained his God-given message, "they were furious and gnashed their teeth at him. … they covered their ears and, yelling at the top of their voices, they all rushed at him, dragged him out of the city and began to stone him." And what did Stephen say while being killed? "While they were stoning him, Stephen prayed, 'Lord Jesus, receive my spirit.' Then he fell on his knees and cried out, 'Lord, do not hold this sin against them.' When he had said this, he fell asleep" (Acts 7:54-60, NIV). Stephen followed the example of the Lord Jesus.

Years later we find the apostle Paul reaching the end of his life. Since his conversion, he had spent his whole life preaching the gospel and helping establish new local churches. When he was being judged and sentenced he found himself alone: "At my first defence no one stood with me, but all forsook me" (2 Timothy 4:16). What a bunch of ungrateful Christians! Paul had invested his life in these people. He had reason enough to feel disappointed and even bitter towards them. But what does Paul say? "May it not be charged against them. But the Lord stood with me and strengthened me" (2 Timothy 4:16-17). The apostle Paul followed the example of the Lord Jesus.

Misunderstandings about forgiveness

Now we shall turn our attention to a number of misunderstandings about forgiveness. Some people say, "Forgiveness? No! It's not fair to forgive. People should

MISUNDERSTANDINGS ABOUT FORGIVENESS

pay for the wrong they have done." Is this correct? When someone has finished paying off his debt with a bank, he is free. He does not need the bank's forgiveness. When a prisoner finishes serving the required five years in jail, he is released. He is free. He has paid the just price so he does not need forgiveness. However, Biblical forgiveness is not about justice, it is an act of grace. God will always take care of justice. It is in His nature to do so. But we, the hurting, the offended, are asked to freely and graciously forgive.

Others say, "To forgive is to forget. And since I shall never forget what he has done to me, I can't forgive." Recall the story you read in the *Foreword*, about a sharp splinter of glass buried deep in someone's arm. Those who do not forgive walk around like that, with a piece of broken glass in their arm. That piece of glass will regularly generate moments of sharp pain that will remind the victim of the accident. A person who has not forgiven will experience an unusually strong reaction when confronted with certain people, attitudes or situations.

What can we do to get rid of this piece of glass? Clean our arm with soap? Use some strong disinfectant? Psychotherapists can help you find out what triggers your pain and will teach you to avoid such situations. If you follow their advice, your pain will be less. But that is not the Christian way. We can do better. The Lord Jesus commands His followers to forgive from the heart, that is, to remove the sharp glass. It will be necessary to cut the arm open again in order to extract the foreign body. Forgiveness is painful! To recall nasty things that others have said or done to you, and then say aloud "I now forgive… I now let him or her go…" – that is painful. But it is necessary to extract that piece of glass so that the wound can heal properly.

Only after genuine forgiveness has taken place can the process of forgetting begin. Shall we ever really forget a serious offence? As long as glass remains in your arm you will experience regular painful reminders of the injury. You will never be able to forget. But once you have forgiven from your heart, the glass is removed. Your arm will begin to heal. In time your arm will recover complete mobility. Some experiences in life we shall never forget. The scar on our arm will always remain visible.

But after you have forgiven from your heart, the pain associated with this memory will begin to decrease. There will come a time when you will feel no pain when you remember the injury. Through forgiveness, the Lord has healed you. Once you choose to obey the Lord Jesus and forgive the offenders with all your heart, that frustration, that anger, that desire for revenge will gradually be replaced by a mixture of sadness, concern, pity and compassion for those who sinned against you.

Some are afraid that if they forgive they open the door for exploitation. "If I forgive these evil people they will continue to hurt me." Yes, that may happen. So after you forgive, you may also need to take some protective measures. One Sunday morning, while we were away at church, some thieves broke into our house in Colombia and took off with a number of items. We forgave those unknown thieves. But I still informed the police and we reinforced the metal bars outside all our windows. After forgiveness it may be appropriate to take some preventive action.

Some people say they will forgive under certain conditions: "I will forgive you if you promise not to do it again." That is not forgiveness. Of course we hope that the offender will repent, or at least not offend again, but our forgiveness should not depend on that. We forgive from our heart without placing conditions. Forgiveness is a gift of grace, and grace is always undeserved. It is free.

Some say that they will forgive when they "feel like it". Their view is that it is hypocritical to forgive our offender when deep inside we don't really feel like forgiving him. But if we wait until we feel a warm desire to forgive, we shall probably never forgive.

To forgive is also an act of obedience! Have you surrendered your life to the Lord Jesus? Is He now the boss, the Lord, the owner of your life? He now commands you to forgive that person who has hurt you. He orders you to forgive with all your heart. What are we now going to do? The only honest alternative is to obey, to act, to forgive – even when it hurts!

FORGIVENESS AND BITTERNESS

Consider Hebrews 12:15. "See to it that no-one falls short of the grace of God and that no bitter root grows up to cause trouble and defile many" (NIV).

One of the consequences of not forgiving is spiritual stagnation. This verse highlights other sad effects. Lack of forgiveness is one of the things that produce a root of bitterness in our heart, and this bitterness will cause trouble and contaminate other people. A bitter wife will influence her husband and children. A bitter man will influence his church and workplace. Bitterness cannot be hidden for long. It will find its way to express itself, and when it does it defiles others.

What if someone says that he just can't forgive? Consider, for example, the story of the young woman who was raped. Perhaps someone has been regularly abused in their youth by a pervert uncle. For some, just the possibility of forgiving makes them feel very angry. "No! I simply cannot forgive that! It is impossible!" If you think it is impossible, you will never do it. But with God's help it is not impossible.

Someone once said to me that if an offence was too difficult to forgive, he would pray, "Lord, you forgive this person because I can't." That is avoiding the issue. That is not obedience. God forgives sinful men and women only when they repent. He knows what He is doing. But He calls on us to forgive from the heart those who sin against us. He also empowers us to obey Him. A better prayer would be, "Lord, I am weak, I feel incapable of forgiving him. Strengthen me; help me to obey You and forgive him." And then, in the name of Jesus, forgive him. God acts in justice. But God expects us to express grace, to obey and to forgive.

Sometimes, after a very serious offence, our mind and emotions may be in such a state of turbulence that we are incapable of taking decisions. We are hurt and confused. Some days or weeks may be necessary before we are 'with it' enough to make decisions again. But if, after weeks go by, we continue saying "I just cannot forgive", we will feel justified in not forgiving. If God commands us to forgive, then forgiveness is possible. It is a decision of the will. We decide to forgive the offender. And we decide to forgive in obedience to the Lord Jesus. But, of course, this is not always easy.

Years ago, when I preached on forgiveness, I would feel satisfied when the listeners understood the message. I felt my task was complete once the listeners understood that forgiveness was necessary in order to grow as a

Christian. But I soon discovered that listeners can understand the message of forgiveness, they can agree with the message of forgiveness, they can rejoice in the message of forgiveness... but they can also go home and not forgive! I decided to change my strategy. Today, when I finish teaching on forgiveness, I frequently create an opportunity to forgive. I encourage a moment of silence where listeners can respond to the promptings of the Holy Spirit, obey and forgive – before they go home. You will also find this opportunity at the end of Part One.

WHEN A BELIEVER CANNOT FORGIVE

Sometimes a Christian can be convinced that he should forgive, he desires to forgive, he may have taken the decision to forgive, but somehow he just can't bring himself to say 'I forgive' – something stops him saying it. I would not have thought this possible until I encountered such a situation myself. One of our new sisters tried to forgive her husband. During the counselling session she began to pray: "In the name of Jesus I f... f... f..." And she couldn't go any further. The words could not leave her lips. It was clearly a spiritual battle. This is a situation where the words in James 5:16 apply: "Confess your trespasses to one another, and pray for one another, that you may be healed." These spiritual battles are real battles, genuine struggles in the spiritual realm.

If it is evident that a believer has a genuine struggle to forgive another, we should come together – two or three brothers or sisters – and pray with the believer until something happens. This sister from our local church in Armenia, Colombia, used to work as a prostitute. About a year after her conversion we suggested some counselling. Together with another brother, we met with her for two hours every Tuesday afternoon.

We talked extensively with her about this issue of forgiveness. She agreed with the Biblical explanations, she agreed that she needed to forgive, and she wanted to do it. She wrote a long list of names of people who had badly hurt her, people she wanted to forgive. We supported her in prayer as, in prayer, she forgave one by one the people on her list. She would pray something like: "I forgive my neighbour Marta for what she did to me five years ago. She screamed at my little daughter and pulled her hair. That made me feel very inadequate as a parent, and so angry. Since then I have hated her." After mentioning the name, she would describe in prayer what that person had done to her. She would say how she felt – this is part of the cutting open the wound in order to remove the glass – and then, if appropriate, she would ask the Lord to forgive her negative reaction or attitude. She would end her prayer with "In the name of Jesus, I let this person go, I forgive him or her."

Working through a list of names can be a long and tiring process. Sometimes the whole process can feel rather mechanical. But don't give up, it works! When we pronounce forgiveness, something really happens! She skipped over the name of her husband and we carried on down her list of names. At the end, of course, we came back to her husband. It was her husband who had forced her into a life of prostitution. She began to pray but could not pronounce his name. To help her, we wrote down the words of the prayer on a sheet of paper. She only had to read and pray them. She tried again and again. She moved back and forth restlessly in her chair. "Do you want to forgive him?" we asked. "Yes", she said, but she could still not pray aloud that simple prayer. We tried together for half an hour. The time was up, so we decided to stop and continue the next week. During the following days, the Colombian brother and I discussed her situation. He suggested that demons were most probably involved in this case, that the sister was being held back by demonic forces. Before the next counselling session, we decided to fast and pray, following the words recorded in Matthew 17:21.

When we met, we talked again about forgiveness. She still wanted to forgive her husband, so we prayed for her and then encouraged her to forgive him in prayer. Again she could not say the words of the prayer. I felt quite frustrated. It was only a short little prayer. She only needed to say aloud, "I forgive him." Why could she not say it? I said to her: "I shall read the prayer slowly, and you simply repeat after me one word at a time." She agreed. And again she got stuck on "I f... f... f..." She could not say the word 'forgive'. After about half an hour of praying and trying, she eventually said the word 'forgive'. Then she got stuck when trying to say the name of her husband. She was no psychiatric patient. A spiritual battle was taking place. After more than an hour, she managed to forgive her husband audibly in prayer. After praying she lifted her eyes up from looking at the floor and looked at us. Her face had changed. It was radiant! This was the first time in nearly the one and a half years that I knew her that she looked at me in the eye. She was always a friendly and rather shy person, but she would avoid eye contact. She had forgiven! She was now free!

We should never condemn a brother or a sister who is finding it difficult to forgive. They may be discouraged and think that they will never be able to forgive. Such people can forgive, but maybe they need the help and support of fellow Christians.

What is involved in forgiving?

What exactly is forgiveness? Forgiveness means to unilaterally cancel a debt. It means to purposefully set aside your own rights. It means to cut a rope that links you to a particular situation, memory or person. Forgiveness is the decision not to hold the sins of another against them.

To forgive does not involve trying to minimize the magnitude of someone's sin. It does not involve trying to find explanations and justifications for the sinner. No! Forgiveness means recognizing the true awfulness of what this person has done, calling it sin, and then, in the name of Jesus, letting this person go free. As we forgive, we decide not to hold on to the sins of another.

Listen carefully, to forgive means to accept living with the negative and painful consequences caused by the sin of another.

Suppose you are riding home on your bike or your motorcycle. As you cross the junction a car does not stop at the red light but drives straight into you. The car is driven by a drunk driver. You are rushed to hospital, and, unfortunately, they must amputate your right leg. Now you have to spend the rest of your life with only one leg. Why? Whose fault was it? It was the fault of this selfish, irresponsible, drunk driver. Every time you move from your bed to the bathroom, every time you drop your soap as you take a shower, every time you see your friends run or play football... you remember that accident. It's not fair. So many events during the day will make you think of that accident, of that careless driver. Your life has been completely changed by this accident. Sometimes you feel depressed. Sometimes very angry. And what about the drunk driver? His insurance paid

WHAT IS INVOLVED IN FORGIVING?

for the cost of the accident. He has bought a new car. His driving license has been returned to him. He has forgotten about the accident. He really does not care about you and your situation. In fact, he may still occasionally drink and drive. His life has returned to normality but your life has been irreversibly damaged. He sinned and you are paying for it. You will suffer the consequences of his careless selfishness for the rest of your life.

What is forgiveness? It means to accept living with the negative and painful consequences caused by the sin of another. "In the name of Jesus I forgive the irresponsible drunk driver! I accept living with the limitation of having only one leg." If you pray forgiving from your heart, you will be set free from the negative emotions generated by this accident. After forgiving you will still only have one leg. But you will be a happy person with one leg! The choice is really quite simple. You have two options. You can either be a bitter person with one leg or you can be a happy person with one leg. The Lord Jesus has redeemed you, He has made you free. He would really like you to enjoy that freedom, even with one leg. Choose to forgive. Accept living with the difficult consequences of another person's sin.

Perhaps you are currently suffering due to the mistakes, the carelessness, the selfishness – the sins of others. Perhaps your mother was a heavy smoker, and you now have problems with your lungs. Maybe you had a very dominant father. He has destroyed your career options by forcing you to study something that never really interested you. Perhaps your son or daughter has chosen to marry the 'wrong' person. Maybe some dominant people have managed to divide your local church. Their wrong decisions and actions have affected you. You hurt now because of them. What are your options? What can you do? You can choose to obey the Lord Jesus and forgive each of them from your heart. This does not mean that you agree with them. The act of forgiving will open the door for joy and freedom, even when the circumstances don't change.

Let's now look at some examples in the Bible of people who did and did not forgive.

People who did not forgive

Mephibosheth

"Jonathan, Saul's son, had a son who was lame in his feet. He was five years old when the news about Saul and Jonathan came from Jezreel; and his nurse took him up and fled. And it happened, as she made haste to flee, that he fell and became lame. His name was Mephibosheth" (2 Samuel 4:4).

This is the story of a young man named Mephibosheth. He could not play football. He had no wheelchair. He had to be lifted on to a donkey and lifted off again. And all this complication in his life was caused by that nurse who dropped him when he was a small boy. I wonder how many times he must have wondered why that woman could not have been just a little bit more careful. He was born healthy. He came from a healthy family. But now he had to live the life of a lame man. Can you imagine those moments of depression and anger as such thoughts circulated again and again through his head?

"So the king said to him, 'Where is he?' And Ziba said to the king, 'Indeed he is in the house of Machir the son of Ammiel, in Lo Debar.' Then King David sent and brought him out of the house of Machir the son of Ammiel, from Lo Debar. Now when Mephibosheth the son of Jonathan, the son of Saul, had come to David, he fell on his face and prostrated himself. Then David said, 'Mephibosheth!' And he answered, 'Here is your servant!' ... Mephibosheth bowed down and said, 'What is your servant, that you should look upon such a dead dog as I?'" (2 Samuel 9:4-8).

King David was looking for the descendants of Saul in order to show kindness for his son Jonathan's sake. It turned out that Mephibosheth was the only one left and now David wanted to find him. But where was Mephibosheth now? In Lo Debar. The name of that place means 'no pasture'. What a sad and depressing situation: a man who was born in a palace, who belonged to the royal family, now lived disabled in a desert, an arid spot with no pasture. Do you think he missed the irony of his hopeless situation? If only this nurse would have done her job properly. Nurses are supposed to look after children, not disable them! "I was not born for this!" "I belong to the royal family but live in misery!" "This is not fair!"

The lack of forgiveness slowly but surely eats away at the human heart. In time it can negatively affect your view of yourself. "What is your servant, that you should look upon such a dead dog as I?" (verse 8). Mephibosheth, a grandson of the first king of Israel, now considers himself a "dead dog". We are all made differently. For some the decision not to forgive will drive their thoughts along the paths of self-pity, low self-esteem and depression. Because of what another has done, "I am now worth less than a dog. In fact, I'm a dead dog – I'm not worth anything!"

JEPHTHAH

Let us look at another example: "Jephthah the Gileadite was a mighty warrior. His father was Gilead; his mother was a prostitute. Gilead's wife also bore him sons, and when they were grown up, they drove Jephthah away. 'You are not going to get any inheritance in our family,' they said, 'because you are the son of another woman.' So Jephthah fled from his brothers and settled in the land of Tob, where a gang of scoundrels gathered around him and followed him" (Judges 11:1-3, NIV).

Here is a man named Jephthah. This man is usually remembered as the one who sacrificed his daughter because she was the first who came to meet him after he came home from a victory in battle (Judges 11:18-40). But in Judges 11 we read about his childhood. Do you think this young man felt comfortable with the thought that his mother was a prostitute? How can children of prostitutes think? "I am not the product of a loving relationship. My father paid for some selfish quick sex, and… here am I! My conception and birth were my mother's 'bad luck.' I am worthless. I am a mistake." For a while Jephthah was allowed to benefit from the comforts of his father's home. But his half-brothers did not accept him. They didn't think he was worthy to receive a share of their father's inheritance. They drove him out of their father's house!

Can you imagine what happened in the heart of this young man? His reaction was different to that of Mephibosheth. His resentment did not lead him to depression but to aggression. He excelled in strength and violence. He attracted a following of scoundrels.

Years later, the elders of Gilead called Jephthah back. They recognized his capacity to fight and wanted him to be their commander against the Ammonites. "But Jephthah said to the elders of Gilead, 'Did you not hate me and drive me out of my father's house? Why have you come to me now when you are in distress?' " (Judges 11:7). One can nearly feel the pain in his voice: "You drove me away." "Your father was also my father." "You drove me away from my father and from my father's house." "I had done nothing wrong, but you hated me." Here is a man with pain who has not forgiven his brothers. He was now a grown man but he had not forgotten the hate of his childhood. He was still tied to the unpleasant history of his family. He sensed a need to prove himself before his brothers. By becoming strong and aggressive he could prove to himself and to others that he was valuable. "I may be the son of a prostitute, but I am a first class warrior." He was not a free man; he was still bound to his childhood problems. Lack of forgiveness affects the way we live. Our decisions are influenced by our painful memories. The Lord Jesus wants us to walk free from our past. He wants us to forgive.

SAMSON

Samson is another unhappy example. "And she [Delilah] said, 'The Philistines are upon you, Samson!' So he awoke from his sleep and said, 'I will go out as before, at other times, and shake myself free!' But he did not know that the LORD had departed from him. Then the Philistines took him and put out his eyes, and brought him down to Gaza. They bound him with bronze fetters, and he became a grinder in the prison" (Judges 16:20-21).

What a sad end for a servant of God. Let us imagine how he must have felt. A large-framed muscular man, a man built for a purpose, a Spirit-filled man, but now blind and chained to a mill, spending his day walking round in circles. He had lost his freedom. He had lost his eyesight. He could no longer wink at the beautiful girls. As he turned the mill round and round in darkness, he became increasingly frustrated, angry and bitter. He began to imagine how he could take revenge.

Samson's last prayer gives us a glimpse into his mind. "Then Samson called to the Lord, saying, 'O Lord God, remember me, I pray! Strengthen me, I pray, just this once, O God, that I may with one blow take vengeance on the Philistines for my two eyes!'" (Judges 16:28). He is willing to die in the pursuit of his goal. And what was his goal? He is not thinking of the future wellbeing of the nation of Israel. He is not thinking of the honour of God nor of fulfilling his divine calling. He is thinking of revenge. "Lord, I am angry because I walk in darkness. They gouged out both my eyes. It is painful. It is humiliating. It is hopeless. I don't want to go on living like this." Samson died a bitter man, seeking revenge for the loss of his eyes.

Can Christians die as bitter men and women? Yes, this is possible! Unfortunately it does happen! But regardless of the pain others have inflicted on us, bitterness is not inevitable. That is the wonderful news! By forgiving from the heart we can break those chains of resentment. We shall then be free to fulfil our Divine calling in life.

In Romans 12:19 we read, "Beloved, do not avenge yourselves, but rather give place to wrath; for it is written: 'Vengeance is Mine, I will repay,' says the Lord." It is not our task to seek revenge. We leave such matters with God.

We can promote the cause of justice without seeking revenge. We may need to report an offence to the police – this may be the responsible thing to do. But we do not do this in order to seek revenge. In the example of rape, which I mentioned earlier, it is perfectly in order for the young woman to report the rape to the police and to cooperate with their investigations. If these two men are caught and sent to prison, they may have time to reflect and change their ways. Their sentencing will be a protection for women in the area and a clear deterrent for other wayward men. All this is compatible with genuine forgiveness from the heart. We may cooperate with the course of justice but it is not our task to seek revenge. We leave such matters with God.

People who did forgive

A Jewish young lady

Now I would like to draw your attention to two beautiful examples. The first example concerns a young Israeli girl who lived in the house of Naaman. "Now Naaman, commander of the army of the king of Syria, was a great and honorable man in the eyes of his master, because by him the Lord had given victory to Syria. He was also a mighty man of valor, but a leper. And the Syrians had gone out on raids, and had brought back captive a young girl from the land of Israel. She waited on Naaman's wife. Then she said to her mistress, 'If only my master were with the prophet who is in Samaria! For he would heal him of his leprosy.'" (2 Kings 5:1-3).

For a moment try to imagine yourself in the shoes of this young lady. Imagine the fear in your small town when rumours spread that a band of armed men from Syria had been seen approaching. Imagine the screams and the panic as these fighters attack – violently destroying all resistance. Among the dead are your parents. For some reason you were not killed but taken captive. You would never forget the weeping, the pleas for mercy, the heat and smoke from burning houses.

After a very long journey, you are handed over to be a maid in the house of your kidnapper, the very one who had led that unfair and evil assault. How would you now feel? She would meet Naaman regularly. His presence, his voice, would bring back so many painful memories. Perhaps she thought of ways to take revenge. Maybe the idea of mixing some poison in his food had crossed her mind.

And what did this young girl do? She forgave Naaman! How do we know? Because of her behaviour. When she heard that Naaman had leprosy, she did not jump up and down with joy. She didn't thank the Lord for a taste of 'sweet revenge'. No! She expressed concern for him. When you forgive, you are set free to bless others, even those who have hurt you. Without forgiveness, she could never have been a blessing to Naaman. Notice that the young girl was not kidnapped as a baby. She was old enough to remember that back home lived a useful prophet, a man of God. She must have remembered many things from back home. The act of forgiving had allowed her emotional wounds to begin to heal. She could still remember what Naaman had done, but without anger, and with less pain. Those who have forgiven can then be used by God to bless others, sometimes even those who have done – or are still doing – much harm.

Joseph

"Joseph said to his brothers, 'I am Joseph; does my father still live?' But his brothers could not answer him, for they were dismayed in his presence. And Joseph said to his brothers, 'Please come near to me.' So they came near. Then he said: 'I am Joseph your brother, whom you sold into Egypt. But now, do not therefore be grieved or angry with yourselves because you sold me here; for God sent me before you to preserve life.' ... Moreover he kissed all his brothers and wept over them, and after that his brothers talked with him" (Genesis 45:3-5, 15).

What a moving story! Do you think Joseph could have received his brothers like this if he hadn't first forgiven them in his heart? Joseph had a collection of very painful memories. The memory of that day when his brothers grabbed him and threw him into a pit. He had cried for mercy but his brothers were in no mood to listen. The memory of the day when his brothers sold him as a slave to some merchants. He had begged them to take him home, but they laughed as they shared the money among themselves. He felt hurt, afraid and lonely. There was not much 'good' he could remember about his childhood years with his brothers. Over the years he had plenty of time to think again and again about these painful experiences.

But the story in Genesis 45 shows us that something important had happened in the heart of Joseph. Were his brothers repentant? Had they confessed their sin to their father? No! Joseph had forgiven without evidence of their repentance. Joseph did not wait for his brothers to say: "Sorry, Joseph, we have sinned by selling you. Please forgive us." Of course, it would have been fantastic if they had said so. In fact, they should have repented and confessed their awful sin. But Joseph did not wait. He did not reason that the harm done to him was too great to be simply forgiven. He forgave! And by forgiving he became a free man. And when we are free, God can use us to bless others.

Steps to Freedom

Dear brother, dear sister, do you want to be free? Do you want to be used by God to bless other people? Then you have to forgive!

When I preach or counsel on this subject, I frequently invite my listeners to follow three simple steps. Perhaps I may now invite you to follow them too.

1. Ask your heavenly Father to work through His Holy Spirit in your mind, to bring to your conscious memory those people who have hurt you and whom you still need to forgive. Write them down.
2. Look at the name or names on your list, and consciously decide that you are going to forgive each one of these people.
3. Pray over each of the persons on your list, one by one. Bring each before the Lord, and then in the name of Jesus forgive them. Let them go.

To help you in this process, I have included two suggested model prayers. There is nothing magical about them. If you want something to happen in the spiritual world, I suggest you use the words of the prayer with honesty and pray to the Lord God with all your heart. The model prayers are simply tools. If you find this difficult, invite a Christian brother or sister that you trust to support you in prayer while you pray and forgive.

First prayer

Dear God and Father, I thank You for speaking to my heart as I have considered the themes covered in this book. I am grateful for Your wonderful and complete forgiveness. I thank You that You know everything about me, even the things that no-one else knows. Thank You that the blood of the Lord Jesus was shed also for me, and that it has made me clean from all my sin. Thank You for completely forgiving such a great debt.

I also thank You that You have made me aware of the importance of forgiving those who have sinned against me. Thank You, Lord Jesus, that You have shown me how to forgive. I am now prepared to obey You and forgive all those who have hurt me. Please bring now to my mind any and every person whom You want me to forgive. Amen.

Now stop and wait in His presence – give Him time to work inside you.

If the Spirit of God has brought one or more names to your mind, write them on a sheet of paper. If in doubt, I suggest you write that name down too. Do not try to justify what these people have done to you. Simply acknowledge that they have sinned against you and against God. Because you are a Christian, because you want to obey your Lord and Master, you are going to forgive them right now. Do not say: "I would like to forgive him" – that is only a good intention. But say, "I forgive him" – that is a real transaction.

Pray individually and specifically for and over each person that you have on your list. You could use words similar to those in the following model prayer. I would recommend you pray out loud, maybe softly but still audibly. It helps to bring into the open an internal conflict.

SECOND PRAYER

- My God and Father,
- Today I want to forgive ... [here use the person's name], because of what he/she has done to me ... [here describe to the Lord in some detail what he/she has done to hurt you].
- And Father, that has made me feel ... [here try to explain to the Lord how you have felt about that person, about their sin and about yourself].
- Father, I now let it all go!
- Father, in the name of the Lord Jesus I forgive ... [here use the person's name].
- I renounce the right I sometimes feel I have to take revenge.
- Please heal my hurting emotions.
- Thank You, Father, that You have now set me free from this burden.
- Heavenly Father, now please bless ... [here use the person's name].
- In the name of the Lord Jesus, Amen!

If the Holy Spirit has not brought anyone to your mind that you need to forgive, relax! Resist the temptation to engage in unhealthy introspection. Use your time to pray for your friends, your brothers and sisters – those who are struggling and are finding it difficult to forgive. Pray that they may receive the strength to speak out these prayers, to obey the command of the Lord and truly forgive from the heart. Pray that God will continue this process of inner healing in every heart.

Part Two

When Should I Forgive?

When Should I Forgive?

Most Christians are convinced that we should follow the example of our Lord Jesus and obey the apostolic teaching and forgive those who offend us. What is not so clear is when we should forgive. Since God offers forgiveness to those who repent, should we only forgive those who repent? Many Christians say they are *willing* to forgive but will not *actually* forgive until the offender recognizes his or her sin, repents and asks to be forgiven. Some would even claim that it is unrighteous to forgive someone if there is no evidence of repentance.

CHOOSING THE RIGHT TIME TO FORGIVE

The Lord Jesus considered the act of forgiving important. He stressed the need to forgive and the serious consequences of not forgiving when He taught His disciples about prayer. In Matthew 6:14-15 we read, "For if you forgive men their trespasses, your heavenly Father will also forgive you. But if you do not forgive men their trespasses, neither will your Father forgive your trespasses" and in Mark 11:25, "Whenever you stand praying, if you have anything against anyone, forgive him, that your Father in heaven may also forgive you your trespasses." These instructions to forgive are not conditional on the repentance of the offender. Jesus did not say "when you stand praying, if your offender comes to you repentant and apologizes, forgive him." Is this a valid argument?

Some Bible students include repentance in their definition of forgiveness. These seek in every forgiveness text a statement or at least a hint of repentance, and if none is present, they conclude that it must be implied. Is this a valid approach? Why should we forgive if the offender does not repent? Is this forgiveness a cheap psychological escape route to avoid the hard work of confrontation?

In other words, *when* should we forgive those who sin against us… at the *beginning*, when we become aware of their sin, when we first feel the pain, anger or disappointment, before we have had the opportunity to seek the offender, before he has repented? Or at the *end*, after we have had the opportunity to contact the offender, after he has become conscious that he has sinned, after he has repented, that is, when the offender sincerely and humbly comes and asks us to forgive him? Does forgiveness come at the beginning or at the end of a reconciliation process?

Possible difficulties

At this point it is worth taking note of two complications. Firstly an academic matter: when Christians talk together about forgiveness, they frequently mean something different. Some understand forgiveness as choosing to ignore or dismiss an offence. Others view forgiveness as a transaction between two persons or as something similar to reconciliation. Before we look at *when* to forgive, we need to be clear as to which definition of forgiveness we are using.

POSSIBLE DIFFICULTIES

The second matter is a practical reality: forgiveness becomes a possibility only when something wrong has happened. In practice, most offenders either:

- are not aware that they have offended someone,
- they do not consider their act as something wrong or sinful,
- they may think they have done something 'good',

or

- they may be hurting or feeling offended themselves.

Furthermore, some offenders have died or cannot be identified or located. The practical reality is that if our definition of forgiveness requires repentance and confession, we shall only forgive a very small fraction of those who sin against us.

Tim formed part of our Christian congregation. He seldom missed a Sunday worship meeting. He would arrive in an interesting electric wheelchair – an attraction to the children. As a young man, soon after he graduated from Oxford University with a degree in mathematics, he was enlisted in the army to support the Allies during the Second World War. He joined a parachute regiment. A year or two later, he was dropped, together with many other Australian soldiers, over France. He was shot at while in the air, hanging helplessly from his parachute, and since then he has been paralyzed from the neck down. Who shot him? He died last year without knowing who had shot him. For close to 60 years no-one admitted the offence, no-one repented, no-one asked to be forgiven. And yet Tim forgave that unknown German soldier. Together with my children, we visited him in his hospital-home. He showed us some of his photos and wartime certificates. We listened to his story. There was no bitterness in his voice. He was healed inside. He was a happy brother in his electric wheelchair.

The timing of forgiveness is not a secondary abstract discussion. It is vital. It determines the way we live, and the way we die!

ONE WORD CAN MEAN DIFFERENT THINGS

Most languages have words that have various meanings. This can be confusing to a person who is beginning to learn the language, but, in time, he will notice that the meaning of a word is usually quite evident from the context. In Dutch, for example, the word 'kwast' can mean (1) a funny person, (2) a paint brush, (3) lemonade or (4) a knot in a piece of wood. Because these meanings are so different, it is usually easy to determine which meaning the speaker has in mind. For example, if we are told that "George is drinking kwast", no-one will conclude that he is a funny person or that he has a paint brush in his mouth!

When a word has different meanings and these meanings are connected, similar or express parallel ideas, more care is needed. For example, the Bible uses the word "salvation" in various related but different ways. You will have noticed that sometimes salvation is presented as something that has already happened to us (Titus 3:5), sometimes it refers to some future event (Romans 5:9), sometimes it is presented as a gift from God (Ephesians 2:8-9) and sometimes as something that should be earned (1 Timothy 2:15). We are also encouraged to "work out our own salvation" (Philippians 2:12). It is the context that will help us determine if "salvation" refers to healing of a sickness, freedom from condemnation, a godly life, life in heaven, deliverance from enemies or something else. In this case, the different meanings of the word "salvation" are clearly distinct from each other but they are also similar, they all refer to being set free from something, they belong to the same range of meanings, the same "idea family".

We shall now discover that the word "forgiveness" also has different but related meanings, it also has an "idea family".

THE BIBLE'S USE OF THE WORD "FORGIVENESS"

Some students suggest that the Bible's definition of forgiveness runs something like: "Forgiveness is the complete restoration of a repentant offender." Clearly this is what God would like to do with every sinner, but this precise definition of forgiveness does not reflect the scope of meanings suggested by the Greek words the Bible uses for forgiveness. It fits some texts well, but does not fit other texts.

The Bible uses four different Greek words when dealing with the idea of forgiving or forgiveness: three verbs and one noun. But each of these four words is also used to describe situations or activities which have a similarity with forgiveness but are not directly connected with an offence. Try to develop a feel for the "family of ideas" connected with the Biblical concept of "forgiveness" as we consider some examples.

1. *aphiemi* (a verb)

This is the word for forgiveness that the Lord Jesus used in Matthew 6:14-15, "For if you *forgive* men their trespasses, your heavenly Father will also *forgive* you. But if you do not *forgive* men their trespasses, neither will your Father *forgive* your trespasses." This word is also used for "remit", "give up a debt", and "cancel a debt". In the parable of the two debtors, "The master of that servant was moved with compassion, released him, and *forgave him the debt*" (Matthew 18:27).

Of the four Greek words, this is the most frequently used. It also carries the idea of "letting" or "letting go". In the Sermon on the Mount, Jesus taught, "If anyone wants to sue you and take away your tunic, *let him* have your cloak as well" (Matthew 5:40). When a fig tree did not produce fruit in three consecutive years, the owner ordered it to be cut down. The gardener however, interceded for the tree saying "*let it* alone this year also, until I dig around it and fertilize it" (Luke 13:8). After Mary poured expensive perfume on Jesus and the disciples began to object, Jesus defended her saying, "*Let* her alone" (John 12:7). Interestingly, this is the same verb our Lord Jesus used when hanging on the cross, "Father, *forgive* them, for they do not know what they do" (Luke 23:34).

2. *apoluo* (a verb)

Many Bible translations use the word "forgive" in Luke 6:37, "Forgive, and you will be forgiven."

This same word is translated as "release" or "let go" (NIV) in the parable of the two debtors, "The master of that servant was moved with compassion, *released* him, and forgave him the debt" (Matthew 18:27) and "release" when Pontius Pilate "*released* Barabbas" (Matthew 27:26).

3. *aphesis* (a noun corresponding to *aphiemi*)

The Lord Jesus used this word in Mark 3:29 when He said, "But whosoever shall speak injuriously against the Holy Spirit, to eternity has no *forgiveness*" (N.Tr.), and the apostle Paul used it in his discourse to the Jews at

THE BIBLE'S USE OF THE WORD "FORGIVENESS"

Antioch, "Therefore, let it be known to you, brethren, that through this Man [Jesus] is proclaimed to you the *forgiveness* of sins" (Acts 13:38). This word carries the ideas of "release", "dismissal", "deliverance", "liberty" and "permit". The Lord Jesus used the same word when He said, "The Spirit of the Lord is upon Me, because He has anointed Me to preach the gospel to the poor. He has sent Me ... to *set at liberty* those who are oppressed" (Luke 4:18).

4. *charizomai* (a verb)

This is the word translated "forgive" in Ephesians 4:32, "*forgiving* one another, just as God in Christ *forgave* you" and in Colossians 3:13, "bearing with one another, and *forgiving* one another, if anyone has a complaint against another; even as Christ *forgave* you, so you also must do." This word is connected with "charis", the word translated "grace". It is used to indicate that something is "granted" or "given freely". This is the word used in Luke 7:21, "And to many blind He *gave* sight" and in Philippians 2:9, "Therefore God also has highly exalted Him [Jesus] and *given* Him the name which is above every name."

The Biblical "idea family" of forgiveness is rich and colourful. It would even expand a little further if we were to study the Hebrew words connected with forgiveness. Sometimes this forgiveness is motivated by the repentance, confession, admission of need or petition on the part of the beneficiary, but this is not always the case. To suggest that one of these is always implied will force the natural interpretation of some Scriptures (Luke 23:34, Acts 7:60). Sometimes the forgiveness is motivated entirely by the giver. As you continue this study, remember that the word "forgiveness" has a rich "idea family".

DIFFERENT TYPES OF FORGIVENESS

We have explored the Biblical "idea family" connected with the words 'forgive' and 'forgiveness'. Another approach to improve our understanding of forgiveness is to look at what happens when forgiveness takes place.

Bible students soon become aware of a couple of apparent contradictions. At conversion, for example, all our sins are forgiven, and yet John urged his Christian readers to "confess their sins" in order to be forgiven (1 John 1:9). Will God forgive the same sin twice? Was the first forgiveness not sufficient? Was it not complete? Some Christians are so hurt and bitter that they have decided not to forgive even if the offender repents. Jesus taught that if they do not forgive, they themselves will not be forgiven by the Father (Matthew 6:15). But hasn't the Father forgiven every Christian *all* their sins at conversion? Is God threatening not to forgive something He has already forgiven? Most Bible students conclude that there are two types or kinds of forgiveness. The first has to do with salvation, the other with fellowship with the Father.

But God is not the only one who forgives. If we look at the different agents (persons or groups) who forgive and what occurs when they forgive we shall notice that there are a number of different types or kinds of forgiveness, or different aspects of forgiveness, or different activities described by the same word "forgiveness". I propose for your consideration seven different types of forgiveness. These are:

    1.   Legal Forgiveness
    2.   Fatherly Forgiveness

DIFFERENT TYPES OF FORGIVENESS

3. Church Forgiveness
4. Governmental Forgiveness
5. Heart Forgiveness
6. Relational Forgiveness
7. Self-Forgiveness

Before we start, please notice that each one of these seven kinds (or aspects) of forgiveness involves *real* forgiveness. They do not represent different standards of forgiveness. Each type of forgiveness has its function and context. This classification is not an academic "game of words", neither does it seek to provide a "feel good formula", nor is it a catalogue of "administrative procedures". In each of these seven kinds of forgiveness, something *real* takes place. Something is set free. Something closes and something new opens. Let's start by looking at the forgiveness God offers and then move on to human forgiveness.

(1) LEGAL FORGIVENESS

When God forgives, He simultaneously expresses grace and satisfies justice. Grace and justice are no small matters. God could not operate on grace alone, He could not simply say, "I love you, sinner, so I forgive you." The well-known text in John 3:16 highlights the high price that had to be paid for our forgiveness: "For God so loved the world that He gave His only begotten Son…" Only the death of Jesus Christ satisfied justice and, on the basis of this satisfied justice, God can now offer His forgiveness to every repentant sinner. We are forgiven and declared righteous.

When we recognize that we are sinners, and repent and trust in the Lord Jesus for our salvation, God declares us forgiven. "In Him [Jesus] we have redemption through His blood, the forgiveness of sins, according to the riches of His grace" (Ephesians 1:7). God can forgive us because justice has been satisfied. God's forgiveness ensures that *all our sins are forgiven* and therefore we shall never be condemned. "And you, being dead in your trespasses… He [God] has made alive together with Him [Christ], having *forgiven you all trespasses*" (Colossians 2:13). "There is therefore now no condemnation to those who are in Christ Jesus" (Romans 8:1). This Legal Forgiveness is a permanent and complete acquittal from guilt and the penalty for sin.

But there is more, God's forgiveness ensures that we are reconciled and at peace with Him. "Therefore, having been justified by faith, we have peace with God through our Lord Jesus Christ" (Romans 5:1). A new relationship is established. We can now enjoy communion with our God and Father.

How to receive God's Legal Forgiveness

For a sinner to benefit from Christ's death at Calvary, repentance is required. The Lord Jesus explained to His disciples that "*repentance* and *forgiveness* of sins should be proclaimed in His name to all nations, beginning from Jerusalem" (Luke 24:47, ESV). A few days later Peter stood up in Jerusalem and urged the crowd: "*Repent* therefore and be converted, that your sins may be blotted out, so that times of refreshing may come from the presence of the Lord" (Acts 3:19). It is clearly stated in Scripture that sinners only benefit from God's forgiveness if they repent.

At conversion God forgives all our sins. We may at that point in time specifically confess to Him a number of sins which are a burden to our souls, but recognition and confession of individual sins is not a requirement for Legal Forgiveness. We are not conscious of many of

DIFFERENT TYPES OF FORGIVENESS

the sins we commit. We forget many others. Detailed confession of our sins is a practical impossibility. Thankfully, God does not require a detailed confession of all our sins. God extends His Legal Forgiveness to those who turn to Him with a sincere and repentant heart.

The road to conversion is simple. We have offended God. The Holy Spirit works in us and makes us conscious of our sinful acts and attitude (John 16:8). It hurts us. We sorrow. "Godly sorrow produces *repentance* leading to *salvation*" (2 Corinthians 7:10). We turn to God for the salvation of our souls with repentant hearts. God recalls the punishment that Christ received at Calvary and declares us completely and forever forgiven. That is Legal Forgiveness. There are no shortcuts. God has no alternative way to offer Legal Forgiveness without Christ's sacrifice and without our repentance. That is why God "commands all men everywhere to repent" and "is longsuffering toward us, not willing that any should perish but that all should come to repentance" (Acts 17:30, 2 Peter 3:9). But what happens when a forgiven Christian sins?

(2) FATHERLY FORGIVENESS

The apostle John, as an old man wrote: "My little children, these things I write to you, so that you may not sin. And if anyone sins, we have an Advocate with the Father, Jesus Christ the righteous. And He Himself is the propitiation for our sins, and not for ours only but also for the whole world" (1 John 2:1-2). Through the years, John must have seen many Christians sin in one way and another. As born again believers, we do not want to sin. Our aim is not to sin. When we do give in to temptation and sin, the joy and harmony of our relationship with the Lord is broken. King David described his experience as follows: "When I kept silent, my bones grew old through my groaning all the day long. For day and night Your hand was heavy upon me; my vitality was turned into the drought of summer. I acknowledged my sin to You, and my iniquity I have not hidden. I said, 'I will confess my transgressions to the Lord,' and You forgave the iniquity of my sin" (Psalm 32:3-5).

Since God has forgiven *all our sins* at conversion, does He have to forgive the same sin again? The forgiveness we have received at conversion is a Legal Forgiveness, it makes us righteous forever; it guarantees our eternal life. When as children we sin and offend our heavenly Father, we require "Fatherly Forgiveness". The basis for this forgiveness is also the death of Christ. The apostle John explained this to his "dear children" when he said, "If we confess our sins, He is faithful and righteous to forgive us *our* sins, and cleanse us from all unrighteousness" (1 John 1:9, N.Tr.). God does not forgive because He is "good and loving" but because He is "faithful and righteous", faithful to His promise and righteous in applying the atoning death of Christ.

When the Lord Jesus washed the disciples' feet, He used this occasion to teach Peter important lessons on humility and service. But the Lord also hinted at the difference between Legal Forgiveness and Fatherly Forgiveness when He explained, "He who is bathed needs only to wash his feet, but is completely clean; and you are clean, but not all of you" (John 13:10). It is this Fatherly Forgiveness that the Lord will withhold from those Christians who choose not to forgive those who offend them (Matthew 6:15).

GOD'S FORGIVENESS IS A MODEL FOR OUR FORGIVENESS

The fact that sometimes the same Greek word is used when God forgives and when humans forgive implies that there are similarities. When God forgives, the eternal destiny of the forgiven person changes. Clearly this does not happen when we forgive. There are, therefore, also differences. The following well-known texts point to a connection between God's forgiveness and our forgiveness.

(1) COLOSSIANS 3:13 "Bearing with one another, and forgiving one another, if anyone has a complaint against another; *even as Christ forgave you, so you also must do.*"

(2) EPHESIANS 4:30-32 "And do not grieve the Holy Spirit of God ... Let all bitterness, wrath, anger, clamor, and evil speaking be put away from you, with all malice. And be kind to one another, tenderhearted, *forgiving one other, just as God in Christ forgave you.*"

What is the point of comparison implied by the "as" and "just as" in these texts? It does not necessarily imply that God's way of forgiving and ours are identical. To forgive "as Christ forgave you" is, on the one hand, an incentive, a reason or a motivation for us to forgive others. This lesson is also taught in the parable of the two debtors (Matthew 18:23-35).

But to forgive "as Christ forgave you" also suggests that we have something to learn about the *way* God forgives. The Greek word for forgiveness used in both these texts is *charizomai*, the word for forgiveness that is connected to the word 'grace' (*charis*). This choice of word suggests that "as", the direction of the comparison, points to an act of grace rather than to a legal transaction. These texts cannot be used to "prove" that *all* our forgiving must be conditional on the repentance of the offender. Rather, we learn that there are rich parallels of grace: God forgives freely and generously, so should we. God forgives all sins, so should we. God forgives and no longer recalls the offence, neither should we.

God is the "righteous Judge" (2 Timothy 4:8). He is the "one … Lawgiver and Judge" (James 4:12, N.Tr.). Justice and its administration are important. God has delegated some aspects of His authority to parents in the home, elders in the Church, rulers and governing authorities in society. You and I may forgive an offence but the offender may still need to be judged by another competent authority. After satisfying a human authority, the offender will still give account of his offence to God. The offender, the victim and the human authority will all give account of their involvement and response to the offence. In fact, "There is no creature hidden from His sight, but all things are naked and open to the eyes of Him to whom we must give account" (Hebrews 4:13). Although God's forgiveness is unique, human forgiveness is real and valid too.

Before we explore the different types of forgiveness granted by human agents, perhaps some may find it useful to consider graphically the different relationships that can break when someone sins.

DIFFERENT RELATIONSHIPS THAT NEED TO BE RESTORED

The lines in the following figures represent normal relationships. In the context of an offence, a Christian offender has four basic relationships. Depending on the type of offence, one or more of these relationships may be damaged. A **bold** line represents a damaged relationship.

DIFFERENT RELATIONSHIPS THAT NEED TO BE RESTORED

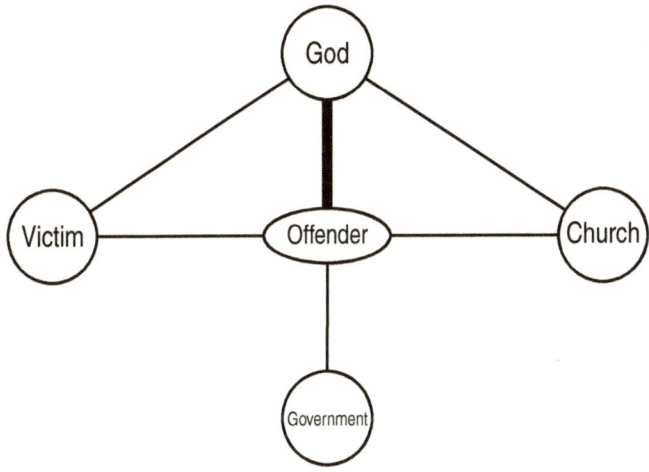

Figure 1: Sometimes we sin only against God. This includes sins in our thought life (Acts 8:22). To restore this broken relationship with God we must confess our sin and receive His forgiveness.

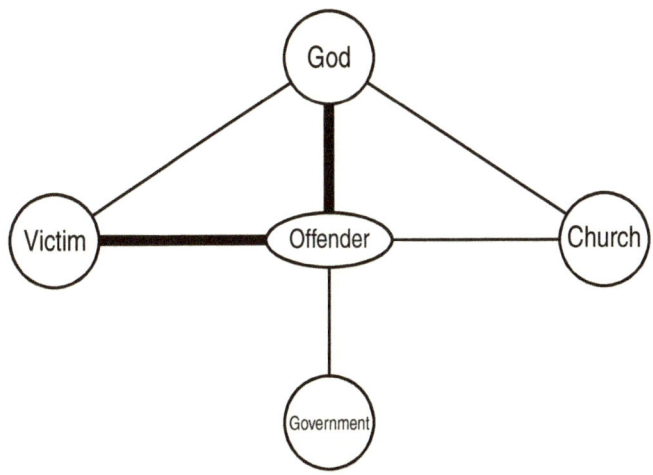

Figure 2: Usually we sin against another person. In this case two of the offender's relationships are broken, that with God and with the victim (Luke 15:21).

THE TRANSFORMING POWER OF FORGIVENESS

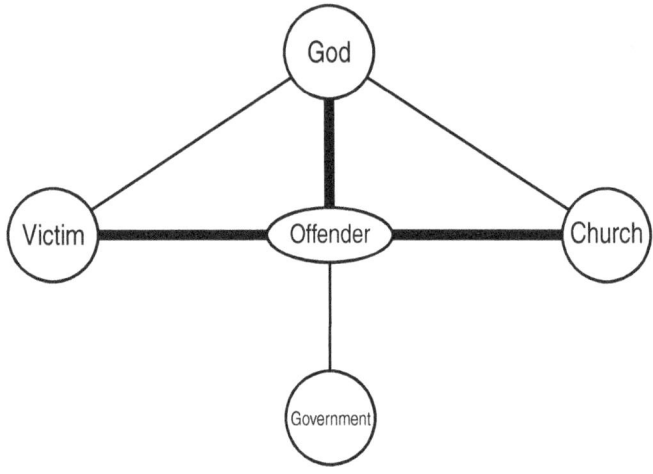

Figure 3: Some of our sins also affect the public testimony of the Church. In this case, not only have the relationships with God and the victim been broken, but also that with the Church (Matthew 18:17).

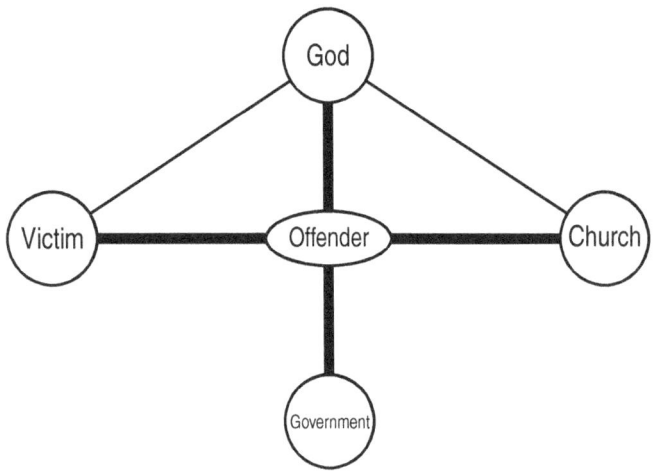

Figure 4: The Government has laws concerning behaviour between people, as well as actions that may not have a direct victim, such as not paying taxes. Some sins

DIFFERENT RELATIONSHIPS THAT NEED TO BE RESTORED

damage the relationship between the Christian and the State. Even after the offender has been forgiven by others, he may still need to pay a fine or go to prison (Romans 13:4).

(3) CHURCH FORGIVENESS

When on earth, the Lord Jesus sometimes publicly forgave sins. For example, "They brought to Him a paralytic lying on a bed. When Jesus saw their faith, He said to the paralytic, 'Son, be of good cheer; your sins are forgiven you'" (Matthew 9:2). Today, the Church, the Body of Christ, is His representative on earth. Sometimes it is the task of the Church to pronounce forgiveness to a repentant believer. The idea here is not that the Church replaces the need of God's forgiveness, but that it acts in harmony with it. Some call this Ecclesiastical Forgiveness, or simply Church Forgiveness.

In certain situations, the Church has been given the task of publicly affirming God's forgiveness. In the context of offending and forgiving, the Lord Jesus taught: "If he refuses to hear them, tell it to the church. But if he refuses even to hear the church, let him be to you like a heathen and a tax collector. Assuredly, I say to you, whatever you bind on earth will be bound in heaven, and whatever you loose on earth will be loosed in heaven" (Matthew 18:17-18). Similarly, to His gathered disciples He said: "Receive the Holy Spirit. If you forgive the sins of any, they are forgiven them; if you retain the sins of any, they are retained" (John 20:22-23).

We see another example of this Church Forgiveness when the apostle Paul urged the Christian assembly in Corinth to forgive a repentant believer: "This punishment which was inflicted by the majority is sufficient for such a man, so that, on the contrary, you ought rather to *forgive* and comfort him, lest perhaps such a one be swallowed up with too much sorrow. Therefore, I urge you to reaffirm your love to him" (2 Corinthians 2:6-8).

(4) GOVERNMENTAL FORGIVENESS

After the flood, God made a covenant with Noah (Genesis 9). As part of this covenant God said: "Whoever sheds man's blood, by man his blood shall be shed" (9:6). Many see here the beginning of human government, since God is delegating to mankind the authority to punish injustice, including the use of the most severe form: capital punishment. The New Testament also presents human government (the State) as God's instrument to maintain justice and punish the evildoer. "Let every soul be subject to the governing authorities. ... The authorities that exist are appointed by God. ... The authority ... is God's minister to you for good. But if you do evil, be afraid; for he does not bear the sword in vain; for he is God's minister, an avenger to execute wrath on him who practices evil" (Romans 13:1-4).

The government's main duty is to execute justice, but it may also, for humanitarian or other reasons, decide to grant a pardon and forgive. Pontius Pilate understood these two functions when he said to Jesus, "Do You not know that I have power to crucify You, and power to release You?" Jesus did not disagree with him. He simply pointed out that Pilate administered authority which he had received "from above" (John 19:10-11). Later Pilate took the decision to crucify Jesus and "released Barabbas" (Matthew 27:26). This is an example of Governmental Forgiveness.

DIFFERENT RELATIONSHIPS THAT NEED TO BE RESTORED

Depending on where we live and what we do, we may be subject to other governing authorities, for example, that of teachers if we are students, that of employers if we work for a company, that of parents if we still depend on them. These may also exercise a form of Governmental Forgiveness.

Although the government, a teacher or a parent may act as God's servant when upholding justice, correcting, punishing or when forgiving, their acts do not replace the acts of God. A person may be forgiven by the State or, after serving a prison sentence, declared 'free' by the State and yet still have matters outstanding with God. God's forgiveness will still be necessary. God's punishment may still follow. God sees the heart and freely forgives but only when sin is acknowledged and confessed (1 Kings 8:39).

(5) HEART FORGIVENESS

When we become aware that someone has sinned against us, something tears in our heart. Our feelings may oscillate between unbelief and anger, disappointment and resentment, depression and desire for revenge. Injustice hurts our hearts badly. This pain in our hearts is very damaging to our spiritual and physical health. It is evident from the teaching of our Lord Jesus that for Him forgiveness was a very serious and an urgent matter. He taught His disciples: "For if you forgive men their trespasses, your heavenly Father will also forgive you. But if you do not forgive men their trespasses, neither will your Father forgive your trespasses" (Matthew 6:14-15). This acid of non-forgiveness, which eats away in our hearts, should be removed as soon as possible.

The ideal is that the offender admits his sin and repents. The goal is reconciliation – the restoration of the broken relationship. But the Lord well knows that in this fallen world such a desirable ideal and such a noble goal may take a long time to become reality and that in many cases (most cases?) it will never be reached. What should we do in the mean time? "... forgive ... from your hearts every one his brother" (Matthew 18:35, N.Tr.). A clean, light and peaceful heart is essential to every form of Christian ministry. Solomon's advice is: "Keep your heart with all diligence, for out of it spring the issues of life" (Proverbs 4:23).

When we recall the injustice committed against us, face the pain it has caused in our heart and pray, forgiving the offender in the name of Jesus, we have forgiven him from our heart. This is no simple psychological trick to avoid the serious work required to serve justice or achieve reconciliation. Heart Forgiveness is usually difficult and very painful but it is what removes the acid, reduces the pain and allows the Lord to begin to heal our wounded soul. Heart Forgiveness ensures that no "root of bitterness springing up cause trouble, and by this many become defiled" (Hebrews 12:15). Heart Forgiveness is the first step in the path towards correction and restoration. Heart Forgiveness cleans our hands and steadies our emotions so that the Lord can use us to remove "the speck in your brother's eye" (Luke 6:41-42).

You may have noticed that the commands urging us to forgive are often connected to teaching about prayer. The presence of non-forgiveness in our heart hinders our relationship with our Heavenly Father and therefore should be removed. If we do not forgive, we shall lose our freedom (Matthew 5:23-25). Sometimes, during a time of prayer, we may recall with pain an outstanding offence. Some injustice committed against us comes to mind. The ideal, as we have seen, is that the offender would admit his sin and repent. The goal is reconciliation. But the offender may live far away, you may not know where to find him, he may be dead... Should you stop praying? Should you suppress the painful memory? What did Jesus say? "And whenever you stand praying, if you have anything against anyone, forgive him, that your Father in heaven may also forgive you your trespasses" (Mark 11:25). This is Heart Forgiveness.

Heart Forgiveness, before the offender repents?

While our Lord Jesus was being crucified, He prayed, "Father, forgive them, for they do not know what they do" (Luke 23:34). This simple and powerful prayer conflicts with many believers' definition of forgiveness. Some suggest that only the Roman soldiers were forgiven. Others that only the specific sin of crucifying Jesus was forgiven (and not all their other sins). Some suggest that this prayer was prophetic for those who later repented when Peter preached (Acts 2:23, 37-41). I get the impression that some Bible students secretly wish Jesus had not uttered forgiveness to unrepentant sinners. It does not comfortably fit in their definition of forgiveness.

But for most, such undeserved forgiveness has become a powerful inspiration. We all admire such a generous act of forgiveness. Leaving aside the controversial 'what happened' question, I think we can all agree that to pray such a prayer while experiencing the agony of death, proves that the Lord Jesus Himself had already forgiven them with all His heart.

THE TRANSFORMING POWER OF FORGIVENESS

The followers of Jesus accepted His teaching on forgiveness and followed His example. As Stephen was being stoned to death, "he knelt down and cried out with a loud voice, 'Lord, do not charge them with this sin.' And when he had said this, he fell asleep" (Acts 7:60). Stephen was not stoned in his sleep! He had just finished delivering a long historical narrative about God's dealings with Israel. He saw the furious eyes of his listeners as he simply told them the truth. He heard them accusing him and soon the crowd were yelling at the top of their voices. Then he felt them grab him and pull him out of the city. They picked up some large stones and begun to stone him to death. It is at this point that he falls to his knees and prays "Lord, do not charge them with this sin." How could he do this? I think we can all agree that to pray such a prayer, while experiencing the agony of death, proves that Stephen, like the Lord Jesus on the cross, had already forgiven them with all his heart.

During his last days, the apostle Paul lived through difficult and disappointing moments: "At my first defence, no one stood with me, but all forsook me." Then he adds, "May it not be charged against them" (2 Timothy 4:16). Notice that these are not expressions of intention. They are not expressing willingness to forgive. They are sincere, painful and unconditional prayers of forgiveness. They are examples of Heart Forgiveness (Matthew 18:35). Church history has many more examples of Christians who forgave those who persecuted, tortured and killed them. Surely such decisions to forgive were not mistakes. Rather, they are clear signs of transformed hearts.

DIFFERENT RELATIONSHIPS THAT NEED TO BE RESTORED

What next?

Forgiveness from the heart makes it possible for us to take the second step of obedience: "Love your enemies, do good to those who hate you, bless those who curse you, and pray for those who spitefully use you" (Luke 6:27-28). After Heart Forgiveness, your indignation, anger and natural desire for revenge (what some would call 'justice') begin to be replaced by feelings of grace, compassion, pity – perhaps even sadness as we consider the miserable state of the unrepentant offender. Unrepentant offenders are usually enslaved and blinded by their own sin. After you have forgiven from your heart, you will notice that your thoughts will change from "what do I want" and "what will make me feel better" to considerations such as "what will help him change for the better", "what does he need right now", "what should I do to protect the offender from hurting others", and "what will most benefit the kingdom of God".

Protecting offenders from the consequences of their sin usually does not help the unrepentant offender. It even may not be helpful for the repentant offender. The point is this: Heart Forgiveness does not eliminate the responsibility to pursue the matter further for the benefit of the offender. The Lord loves the offender and wants to restore him. Sometimes the Lord will make it clear that after Heart Forgiveness the next step is to let the matter rest (1 Corinthians 6:7). But usually the Lord wants to use the one who has been offended to help the offender come to his senses (Matthew 18:15-17). The correct and responsible thing to do may be to report the husband's violence to the Social Services, to report the child molester to the police or dismiss the dishonest worker from the company. The big and important difference is that after I have forgiven from my heart, I can report the offender to the Social Services or to the police without anger in my heart. I can fire the dishonest employee not out of frustration or revenge, but because I am convinced that in the long term this action will benefit the offender most.

I have noticed that many Christians try to follow the procedure in Luke 17:3 ("rebuke him") and Matthew 18:15 ("tell him his fault") before they have forgiven the offender from their heart. Their hurt emotions, their anger, their frustration, their bitterness, their desire for personal justice will find a way of hindering a constructive dialogue. One incorrect reaction from the offending person and the problem will grow even bigger. Only after we have forgiven from our heart shall we be clean and sensitive instruments in the Master's hand as He seeks to work in the soul of the offender.

(6) Relational Forgiveness

Forgiveness from the heart is the unconditional first step in all offence situations. But Relational Forgiveness is conditional on the repentance of the offender. It involves communicating your forgiveness to the repentant offender. Some refer to this as Verbal, Granted, External, Social or Reconciliation Forgiveness. It involves the Lord, the victim and also the offender. Relational Forgiveness to be worth anything must follow (or coincide with) Heart Forgiveness. The healing of the *victim's* hurting heart begins when he forgives the offender from his heart. The healing of the *offender's* guilty and hurting heart begins when he confesses his sin to the Lord and receives God's forgiveness. The healing of the *victim-offender relationship* begins when the offender confesses his sin to the victim and receives the victim's forgiveness.

An atheist offender may repent and seek the forgiveness of his victim without seeking God's forgiveness. When a Christian victim communicates his forgiveness to this repentant offender, the victim-offender relationship will begin to heal even though the offender is still not reconciled to God.

Saying "I forgive you"

When should we tell the offender that we have forgiven him? When should we offer Relational Forgiveness? Normally this should be when the offender repents and asks to be forgiven. But it is worth taking note that the Scriptures do not supply us with a general answer to cover all situations. For the timing, you and I will need to seek guidance from the Lord.

There may be some exceptional situations where it is very helpful for unrepentant offenders to hear that you have forgiven them. Why did the Lord Jesus on the cross audibly express forgiveness? Why did Stephen express his Heart Forgiveness to those who were stoning him? After forgiving in our heart, we shall be prepared to communicate that forgiveness when we hear that the offender has repented or as soon as the Holy Spirit makes it clear to us that it will be beneficial to the offender or the kingdom of God.

Consider, for example, the positive effect of a public offer of forgiveness by the parents of a missionary murdered by Muslim radicals. Their public expression of forgiveness for the unrepentant murderers sends a clear, deep and powerful message of God's grace to the Muslim world.

Consider a situation where a carnal, spiteful sister in your congregation spreads her suspicion that your partner has been unfaithful to you. The circulation of this lie has caused much pain to you and your family. You have taken the heart decision to forgive her and have encouraged your family to do the same. Together you will express that Heart Forgiveness with undeserved acts of kindness towards this carnal sister. But to verbally express forgiveness to her without her acknowledgement of sin and repentance may not be helpful to her. She, and those who believe her lies, will probably understand your offer of forgiveness as an act of manipulation. Saying "I forgive you" or "I have forgiven you" is part of Relational Forgiveness and should normally, but not necessarily always, follow the repentance of the offender.

When not to hold back Church and Relational Forgiveness

We humans usually find the act of forgiveness difficult and painful. Sometimes we feel the repentant offender is not repentant enough, that he is not really aware of the pain he has caused. Sometimes we question the sincerity of the repentant offender, especially if he repeats the offence again and again. This is not a modern struggle! The Lord Jesus, who is head of the Church and Lord of our lives, gave us some very practical instructions. Let's look at these two texts in turn.

(1) LUKE 17:3-4 "Take heed to yourselves. If your brother sins against you, rebuke him; and if he repents, forgive him. And if he sins against you seven times in a day, and seven times in a day returns to you, saying, 'I repent,' you shall forgive him."

Consider carefully what this verse affirms and what it does not affirm. In verse 3 the Lord Jesus makes it clear that He is considering the case when a "brother" sins. It is a pastoral text to be used within the Christian community. The immediate context, verses 1 and 2, confirms that the subject matter is a *general sin*. In other words, if a fellow believer sins, we as a community should express our concern for our brother, confront him and seek his restoration. Once he repents, we restore him to the fellowship of believers: he is declared forgiven. This is Church Forgiveness. Then, in verse 4, the Lord Jesus highlights the situation in which it is most difficult to administer this disciplinary act correctly: suppose now that the brother's sin happens to be specifically "against you", and that the sin is not carried out just once but is repetitive, "seven times". He concludes that the confrontation and restoration procedure should be the same. It should not be influenced by personal pain nor by personal impatience or frustration.

This text, therefore, has a clear mandate: if a fellow believer falls in sin, we should approach him. Once he repents, we should not hold back Relational and Church Forgiveness. Notice that this text does not prescribe how we should deal with offending unbelievers. Neither does it prescribe what we should do if the offender is dead, cannot be contacted or does not recognize that he has sinned. The text affirms only the positive: that a repentant brother should be forgiven. It does not affirm the negative: that an unrepentant person should not be forgiven. For guidelines as to what to do with an unrepentant person we should look elsewhere in Scripture.

(2) MATTHEW 18:15-17 "If your brother sins against you, go and tell him his fault between you and him alone. If he hears you, you have gained your

brother. But if he will not hear, take with you one or two more, that 'by the mouth of two or three witnesses every word may be established.' And if he refuses to hear them, tell it to the church. But if he refuses even to hear the church, let him be to you like a heathen and a tax collector."

As with the previous text, consider carefully what this verse says and what it does not say. It is considering the case when a "brother sins against you". It is a fairly private matter and therefore we are encouraged to seek a solution "between you and him alone". Others are invited to help only because the private explanations and pleadings have proved unsuccessful.

This text has a clear mandate: if a fellow believer sins in such a way that we are personally hurt or disadvantaged, we should approach him. Once he repents, we should not hold back our forgiveness. We have "gained our brother". Notice that this text does not prescribe how we should deal with every type of sin among believers. Not all sin, for example, should be handled just between two. Neither does it prescribe what to do with offending unbelievers, or if the offender is dead or cannot be contacted. The text states a positive: take the initiative and try to "gain" the offending brother. Involve others only if it is helpful and necessary.

The text also affirms a negative: if the offending brother insists in behaving like a unbeliever, he should be treated as an unbeliever. That is, we should treat him with respect but also exclude him from privileges within the Christian community. The accompanying prayer is that the pain caused by exclusion would cause him to come to his senses, repent and be restored. "Brethren, if a man is overtaken in any trespass, you who are spiritual restore such a one in a spirit of gentleness, considering yourself lest you also be tempted. Bear one another's burdens, and so fulfill the law of Christ" (Galatians 6:1-2).

RECONCILIATION

Our heavenly Father specializes in reconciliations. We are told that, "You, who once were alienated and enemies in your mind by wicked works, yet now He has *reconciled* [to God] ..." (Colossians 1:21). Our God is pictured as the loving and generous father who runs towards his repentant prodigal son, embraces, kisses, forgives and then celebrates. In this parable, the Lord describes a celebration in which the forgiven son participates with new clothing, new shoes and a (family?) ring on his finger. The whole household is invited to share a good meal, music and even dancing (Luke 15:20-24). Perhaps we can identify a little with the frustration of the eldest brother. The repentant prodigal son should be forgiven, but why such an extravagant reception? Shouldn't the celebration wait for a few months or years until the prodigal son has *proven* the sincerity of his repentance? Is Relational Forgiveness the same as reconciliation?

The apostle Paul defines the message of reconciliation as, "God was in Christ reconciling the world to Himself, not imputing their trespasses to them" (2 Corinthians 5:18-19). Clearly forgiveness and reconciliation are connected. Our goal is not only forgiveness but, where possible, reconciliation – the complete restoration of a broken relationship (Matthew 5:23-24). Quite often Relational Forgiveness allows immediate reconciliation. On expressing forgiveness the hindrance to reconciliation has been removed and a *full celebration* can begin.

A GROWING CELEBRATION

But counsellors also encounter extremely difficult situations where trust has been seriously and repeatedly abused, and where the emotional damage has been deep. The victim may have forgiven from his heart. The wounds in his soul are healing but have not yet completely healed. Consider situations such as child abuse, adultery or murder. What should the Christian victim do if the offender repents and seeks his forgiveness? Forgive. Is this possible? Yes. But unless there has already been a victory in that painful internal struggle between the urges of his flesh (anger, revenge, get-even) and his desire to obey the Lord's command and forgive, it will be virtually impossible to look some offenders in the eye and sincerely say "I forgive you." Heart Forgiveness prepares the way for Relational Forgiveness. But there may still be no desire to celebrate.

Once forgiveness has been offered by the victim and received by the repentant offender, the hindrance to reconciliation has been removed. In other words, the reconciliation process has begun. With humans, healing and the re-establishment of trust are growing processes. They take time. Our *celebration* begins with Relational Forgiveness and grows towards *full celebration* as the relationship heals.

Here we notice another difference between God's forgiveness (Legal and Fatherly) and our forgiveness (Heart and Relational): reconciliation and celebration always follow immediately when we repent and are forgiven by our Heavenly Father. At that very moment full communion is established, celebrated and enjoyed. Frequently this is also the case when we Christians forgive, but sometimes the celebration and enjoyment may take some time.

RECONCILIATION, FORGIVENESS AND JUSTICE

Our God loves justice. Is it possible to forgive and experience reconciliation without correcting an injustice? A number of Christians at Corinth disagreed seriously with each other. Each party felt strongly that they were in the right, and decided to pursue justice in court. The apostle Paul put this matter in perspective. He wrote:

> 1 CORINTHIANS 6:1-7 "Dare any of you, having a matter against another, go to law before the unrighteous, and not before the saints? ... I say this to your shame. Is it so, that there is not a wise man among you, not even one, who will be able to judge between his brethren? But brother goes to law against brother, and that before unbelievers! Now therefore, it is already an utter failure for you that you go to law against one another. Why do you not rather accept wrong? Why do you not rather let yourselves be cheated?"

The fact that we Christians are born again and have the Spirit of God within us does not eliminate the possibility of sinful behaviour. We can and do sometimes treat each other unfairly. We can hurt each other badly. In harmony with the teaching of the Lord Jesus, the apostle Paul encourages fellow believers to talk together and resolve their differences. If progress stagnates, seek the help of wise and respected believers among you. The main concern of the apostle in this text is not fairness or personal justice but the testimony of the Christian community in the eyes of the unbelieving world.

Where possible, we should seek a balanced and fair solution. But if the offending believer is carnal, immature or simply does not understand or agree with our point of view, the apostle recommends letting go: "Why not rather be wronged? Why not rather be cheated?" Not because you are unable to fight, not because justice has been achieved, not because the offender shows repentance... but out of a higher motivation – the interests of the Lord Jesus on earth. Because we love the Lord Jesus and desire to promote the Kingdom of God, we agree to suffer loss with peace in our heart. This peace and genuine expressions of brotherly kindness are possible if we have forgiven from our heart. Reconciliation, however, will require Relational Forgiveness.

(7) SELF-FORGIVENESS

This type of forgiveness is closely related to Fatherly Forgiveness and Relational Forgiveness. When we confess our sin to the Lord, He forgives. How do we know? Because He has promised to do so. We must learn to believe His promise and accept His forgiveness. Similarly, when we have repented from our sin against another and the offended party has forgiven us, we must learn to accept their forgiveness.

The story of Joseph and his brothers illustrates this well. Joseph forgave his brothers for selling him into slavery but the brothers were unable to accept that forgiveness. How do we know? Because they remained suspicious of him and afraid of possible vengeance. "When Joseph's brothers saw that their father was dead, they said, 'Perhaps Joseph will hate us, and may actually repay us for all the evil which we did to him.' So they sent messengers to Joseph, saying, 'Before your father died he commanded, saying, "Thus you shall say to Joseph: 'I beg you, please forgive the trespass of your brothers and their sin; for they did evil to you.'"'" (Genesis 50:15-21). On hearing this, Joseph wept. It saddened him that his brothers had lived all these years near him but doubting the genuineness of his forgiveness.

But Self-Forgiveness is still something different from accepting the forgiveness offered by others. A father may confess his sin of having neglected his children in order to advance his career. He may accept gratefully the forgiveness offered to him by God, his wife and his children. And yet, he may still hate himself for having neglected his children. Every time he sees a happy family enjoying a barbeque or playing together, pain strikes in his heart. He knows he has been forgiven by God and his family, and yet his heart is not at rest: he has not forgiven himself.

One of Satan's descriptive names is "the accuser of our brethren" (Revelation 12:10) because day and night he highlights the sins of the saints. In most situations, we forgive ourselves at the same time as we receive God's Fatherly Forgiveness. It is wonderful when those we have offended also forgive us. But sometimes they may distrust us, judge the sincerity of our repentance and refrain from forgiving us. Do not judge them. Do not pressure them. Pray for them, live a repentant lifestyle and let the Holy Spirit do His work. The reason we can forgive ourselves is because our heavenly Father has forgiven us. Self-Forgiveness is based on Fatherly Forgiveness and not on Relational Forgiveness.

If after we accepted God's forgiveness and, if offered, also accepted the forgiveness of those we have offended, we still experience moments of painful remorse, hatred and bitterness in our hearts against ourselves, we must learn to forgive ourselves. If you are currently struggling in this area, may I encourage you to enter the Lord's presence through prayer and thank Him again for His full and complete forgiveness for that sin that still torments you. Visualize yourself as that repentant prodigal son being accepted, embraced and completely forgiven by the happy Father. Then, in the Lord's presence, say "In the name of Jesus I now forgive myself for having done…" Learn to graciously forgive yourself and also to believe, accept and rejoice in that forgiveness.

I have summarized the different types of forgiveness and their effects in the following table.

SUMMARY TABLE

Kinds or aspects of forgiveness	Who are involved?	This forgiveness frees us from…	This forgiveness frees us to…
1. Legal Forgiveness	God offender	Eternal condemnation	Enjoy the assurance of our eternal salvation
2. Fatherly Forgiveness	God offender	Broken communion with God. Hypocritical living	Enjoy communion with God
3. Church Forgiveness	God church offender victim (+)	Painful exclusion from expressions of fellowship	Enjoy full acceptance in the Christian community
4. Governmental Forgiveness	God (+) Government offender victim (+)	Paying a fine, prison sentence or some other consequence	Enjoy normal life in society
5. Heart Forgiveness	God victim	Pain, aggressiveness, anger, desire for revenge, self-pity, depression, bitterness	Enjoy inner peace, experience grace, pray, be a blessing to others [The victim begins to heal]
6. Relational Forgiveness	God victim offender	A broken relationship	Enjoy reconciliation [The broken relationship begins to heal]
7. Self-Forgiveness	God self	Painful remorse, self-hate, depression, bitterness	Enjoy inner peace, experience grace, embrace life with joy

(+) sometimes involved

© Philip Nunn, 2009

Conclusion

If you have read carefully through Part One and studied Part Two, you should now have a clearer understanding of what the Bible teaches about forgiveness. As a Christian you are aware and very thankful that your big debt with God has been completely cancelled. You are also aware that God now calls us to forgive from our heart those who have hurt and offended us. What next? What are you going to do with this information? Please don't put this book in a box or back on the shelf. Leave it visible next to your bed or on your desk as a reminder to act – until you do what the Lord is asking you to do.

1. Perhaps you are aware that you have offended another. What can you do? Seek forgiveness. Write that letter, send that e-mail, make that phone call or make that visit. Respond and you will be set free.

2. Perhaps you are aware of pain or even bitterness in your heart against someone who has hurt you. What can you do? Forgive from your heart. Use the model prayer suggested at the end of Part One. Choose to obey God's word: "As Christ forgave you, so you also must do" (Colossians

CONCLUSION

3:13). In the name of Jesus, remove that glass from your arm today! Only then will the pain begin to reduce, only then will you be in a condition to help the offender, only then will God be able to use you to bless others. Respond and you will begin to be healed.

3. Perhaps you are now aware of signs of bitterness in others caused by some stagnant conflict in your family or local church. What can you do? Have you found something in this book that you could use to promote forgiveness and reconciliation? God is active in the reconciliation business. Once we are at peace with God and our fellow humans, He wants to use you and me as His agents to explain and encourage forgiveness and reconciliation (2 Corinthians 5:18-20). Respond and God will use you to bless others.

"Do not merely listen to the word, and so deceive yourselves. Do what it says."
James 1:22 (NIV)

"Blessed are the peacemakers, for they shall be called sons of God."
Matthew 5:9

www.ingramcontent.com/pod-product-compliance
Lightning Source LLC
Chambersburg PA
CBHW032207040426
42449CB00005B/480